The Artful Read-Aloud

The Artful Read-Aloud

10 Principles to Inspire, Engage, and Transform Learning

REBECCA BELLINGHAM

HEINEMANN • Portsmouth, NH

Heinemann

361 Hanover Street

Portsmouth, NH 03801–3912

www.heinemann.com

Offices and agents throughout the world

The author and publisher wish to thank those who have generously given permission to reprint borrowed material:

Excerpt from an interview with Halley Feiffer in *A Funny Thing Happened on the Way to the Gynecological Oncology Unit at Memorial Sloan Kettering Cancer Center of New York City Playbill*. Copyright © 2017 by the Geffen Playhouse. Reprinted by permission of the Geffen Playhouse.

Acknowledgments for borrowed material continue on page x.

Library of Congress Cataloging-in-Publication Data

Names: Bellingham, Rebecca L., author.

Title: The artful read-aloud : 10 principles to inspire, engage, and transform learning / Rebecca L. Bellingham.

Description: Portsmouth, NH : Heinemann, [2019] | Includes bibliographical references.

Identifiers: LCCN 2019029198 | ISBN 9780325109169

Classification: LCC LB1573.5 .B55 2019 | DDC 372.45/2—dc23

LC record available at https://lccn.loc.gov/2019029198

Editor: Zoë Ryder White

Production: Vicki Kasabian

Interior and cover designs: Suzanne Heiser

Interior photographs: Sherry Day

Video crew: Sherry Day, Alan Chow, Dennis Doyle, Michael Grover, and Paul Tomasyan

Typesetter: Kim Arney

Manufacturing: Steve Bernier

Printed in the United States of America on acid-free paper

23 22 21 20 19   CGB   1 2 3 4 5

To Annabelle and Ezra

Raising and reading to you are the joys

of my life. I hope you discover the world, and

yourselves, in the books that will light your way.

I love you to the moon, the stars, and the

galaxies beyond and back.

Contents

Video Contents

HOW TO ACCESS ONLINE RESOURCES

To access the online resources for *The Artful Read-Aloud*:

1. Go to **http://hein.pub/ArtfulReadAloud-login**.

2. Log in with your username and password. If you do not already have an account with Heinemann, you will need to create an account.

3. On the Welcome page choose, "**Click here to register an Online Resource**."

4. Register your product by entering the code: **artread** (be sure to read and check the acknowledgment box under the keycode).

5. Once you have registered your product, it will appear alphabetically in your account list of **My Online Resources**.

Note: When returning to Heinemann.com to access your previously registered products simply log into your Heinemann account and click on "**View my registered Online Resources**."

Acknowledgments

O wonderful, wonderful, and most wonderful wonderful!
And yet again wonderful . . .

—WILLIAM SHAKESPEARE, *AS YOU LIKE IT*

I've always loved this line. It seems to be the most jubilant of phrases, a perfect expression of delight and abundance. I think of that line now as I write my acknowledgments, my deepest expressions of gratitude to the most wonderful, wonderful, and yet again wonderful people who have guided me on my path, who have offered such generosity of time and support, and who have been central to this book-writing journey. I hope I find the sufficient words to say thank you, thank you, and yet again thank you.

Thank you, thank you, and yet again thank you to Lucy Calkins and all the amazing thinkers, book lovers, and literacy leaders at the Teachers College Reading and Writing Project. Lucy, thank you for always honoring my attempts to live out my dreams as an artist and an educator—and for helping me see that my work in both worlds was better and richer as a result. This book and the ideas I tried to bring to life inside of it would never have been possible were it not for the years I spent learning from you. Your wisdom and mentorship live inside of me always. I feel so lucky my path crossed with so many of the staff developers and leaders at TCRWP—in every interaction with each of you, I learned about teaching and learning, children, writing, books, and best practice in balanced literacy. You are extraordinary people!

Thank you, thank you, and yet again thank you to my colleagues in the Literacy Specialist Department at Teachers College. Marjorie Siegel, thank you for championing my arts-based reading course at Teachers College every year, which allowed me to try out many of the ideas inside this book. Our conversations have fueled my passion for teaching with true engagement and artistry. Your mentorship and support have been invaluable to me. Maria Paula, thank you for being an early reader of this book and always being such a thoughtful, generous colleague. Ellen Ellis, your close friendship and genuine love for children are as true as it gets. I've learned so much from you.

Thank you, thank you, and yet again thank you to the school communities, educators, and leaders who have taught me what beautiful, artful teaching looks like, who have inspired me with their passion, commitment, and brilliance, and who have opened their classrooms and their hearts to this work. Thank you to the leaders of the San Diego Unified School District; your dedication to your students and your schools is inspiring. Thank you to Sylvia Ferrer-McGrade, Carol Shirley, and Carolyn Repaire at Adams Elementary and to Kathy Lorden and Dennice Rousey at Grant Middle School. Thank you all for being so committed to this project and for making space for me to work with and read aloud to your amazing first-, fourth-, sixth-, and seventh-grade students. Your classrooms are shining examples of what artful teaching looks like. Thank you to my colleagues at the Shady Hill School, Mott Haven Village School, and Berkeley Carroll School—I would not be the person or the teacher I am were it not for all the hours I spent in conversation with you, inside and outside our classrooms. Thank you to Francis Parker School for being a new home out west; collaborating with you has been a true joy. And finally, thank you to Jacqui Getz, principal extraordinaire. No one exemplifies artful living and leading more than you. Your friendship means the world.

Thank you, thank you, and yet again thank you to the artists and arts organizations who taught me how to live like an artist, who gave me courage to create, and who shine such a bright light in our world and in our classrooms. Thank you to Tim Lord and Jason Duchin, founders and leaders of Dreamyard. The years I spent collaborating, creating, and connecting with you and my fellow teaching artists made everything else possible. Dreamyard is at the center of my artist heart. Thank you to Barbara Retzko, Lowry Marshall, Kathryne

Jennings, Marishka Wierzbicki, and Charlie Alterman. I marvel at all your artistic gifts and feel so grateful to have learned from you.

Thank you, thank you, and yet again thank you to my beloved friends and extended family on both coasts, all of whom have supported me in countless ways throughout my life and in the process of writing this book. Emily Jane, I love the memories of reading aloud to you when you were little. I am so grateful to have such a supportive sister and fellow artist in you! And to my friends at Kettle and Stone, thank you for making the most delicious coffee and giving me an office away from home virtually every writing day of this past year!

Thank you, thank you, and then again thank you to Pam Allyn, founder of LitWorld and World Read Aloud Day. Pam, your belief that this book should come into being helped me stay hopeful. Thank you for believing in me and for believing in the magic of reading aloud. Your fierce advocacy for children has opened a world of imagination and book joy for so many girls and boys around the world.

Thank you, thank you, and yet again thank you to the spectacular Heinemann team, who bring such expertise and generosity to everything they do. I was blown away by your dedication to this project. Thank you, Jamie Hudson, for starting the chain of events. What serendipity to meet you! Thank you to the amazing production team for their careful and thoughtful direction: Sherry Day, Michael Grover, Dennis Doyle, Allen Chow, and Paul Tomasyan. What a treat to spend three days in classrooms together! Thank you to all the brilliant people who are part of the marketing, editorial, and design team: Elizabeth Silvis and team; Brett Whitmarsh and team; Catrina Marshall; and Vicki Kasabian, Elizabeth Tripp, and Suzanne Heiser. I am in awe of your beautiful work on this project.

And, thank you, thank you to Zoë Ryder White—you are an editor of anyone's dreams. To be able to trust someone so completely with all my ideas and my first-draft attempts was a gift of a lifetime. I cannot thank you enough for partnering with me in this process and for shaping this book into something I want to share with the world. Thank you for shepherding me through this writing journey with such grace and encouragement and for becoming a true friend to boot!

And finally, thank you, thank you, and yet again thank you to my family, my Lark Street team, and the heart of my heart.

To my parents, who raised me to love books and ideas, to listen and live with wonder and gratitude. You are my reading (and teaching!) heroes, you are my pals, and you are my favorite people in the world. I am so grateful to you for paving the way and reading the world alongside me.

To my little noodlebugs, your spirits are a miracle. As I was writing this, I was interrupted by you both as you burst into my office to squeal, "Mommy!" and give me a tight squeeze and a juicy kiss on my face. Nothing could top that. No one could top you. Thank you for being the most wonderful, wonderful, and yet again wonderful children.

And finally, to Ben, thank you for being not only my partner in all things but my truest champion. Your belief in me is so genuine and so unwavering—you keep me balanced and you keep me laughing. I love you so much for always checking in, for allowing me to dream, and for believing in the power of books and reading aloud as much as I do, as evidenced by your very artful read-alouds each night to Annie and Ezra! Marrying the book-loving soul you are was the wisest decision I ever made.

Introduction

You need intelligence, and you need to look. You need a gaze, a wide gaze, penetrating and roving—that's what's useful for art.

—TONI MORRISON

Toni Morrison's description of what's useful for art—intelligence, a penetrating and wide gaze, and a desire and capacity for looking and noticing—is a beautiful summation of what I find useful for reading aloud to children. Without fail, every time I've shined a spotlight on the importance of reading aloud and the artful, instructional moves inside an effective interactive read-aloud, teachers and graduate students have told me how much it affected them, how they changed their practice, or how they made room for reading aloud in their classrooms. They often tell me it completely shifts the dynamics of their classrooms: that children's passion for books and stories skyrockets, their conversations about characters and stories lead to more inclusive, thoughtful communities, and kids read their own independent books with more vigor and commitment.

Several years ago, one of my graduate students in the Literacy Specialist Program at Teachers College said to me, "You should just become the queen of read-aloud!" Of course I laughed at this idea (and also sort of enjoyed the idea of being the queen of something!), but it planted a seed: I should write a book about everything I had learned about reading aloud from the stance of both an educator and an artist. I should write a book that would make it possible for teachers to give children one of the most important gifts an educator can give: access to the power and wonder of story.

I started my career as a teaching artist in New York City, working with the Dream-yard Project, a community arts organization that places artists in long-term residencies in public schools. At the time I was also a working actress. In between auditions, rehearsals, and sometimes eight shows a week, I integrated theatre and music into multiple curricular areas in several schools across the South Bronx. I directed plays, musicals, choirs, and Shakespearean performances. I helped develop original plays and performances using the stories, poems, and ideas of children in kindergarten through eighth grade. For most of these children, my fellow teaching artists and I were the art departments in their schools. Most of the time, they didn't have school-based music or drama classes, and they certainly didn't have budgets for annual shows where kids could perform onstage and experience the singular magic of putting on a show together.

My cadre of teaching artists, classroom teachers, and I produced many works of art on a shoestring budget. We didn't have spotlights or fancy costumes. We had the simplest of tools: our voices, our bodies, our understanding of color and space, our imaginations, and our ability to make something beautiful simply by singing, speaking, and moving as an ensemble. And we had words—from books, plays, and the students themselves. We had words that felt thrilling or hilarious. We had words that told stories of great courage or great treachery and that taught us how to help one another in times of need. Most importantly, we had the glorious imaginations and open hearts of the children with whom we worked. The combination of those words and the children's joyful capacity for expressing them made it possible to make magic.

What we had were things every teacher has access to. We had great stories to tell and groups of children eager to hear those stories and bring them to life. After many years of working as a teaching artist and eventually a classroom teacher, literacy coach, and instructor, I started thinking more and more about how to help teachers use the tools artists have long used to spark engagement, connect deeply, provoke inquiry, and inspire deep thinking. And I began with the time of day that has always been my favorite as a classroom teacher, literacy coach, graduate-level instructor, and mom: the read-aloud.

While most teachers do daily read-alouds and believe in their importance, there are moves we can make to significantly elevate the instructional power of reading aloud.

For instance, making small shifts with our bodies and voices can help kids envision different characters and their actions more completely. Slowing down, creating silences, and being aware of pacing can help kids begin to understand that certain passages hold key information and are worth rereading and lingering over. Making intentional eye contact with students during pivotal scenes between characters helps students infer the emotions, consider the significance of moments across the book, or simply feel utterly drawn into the story. Each of these moves is also artistic in nature: embodiment, breath, and connection are at the center of almost every artistic endeavor, and they can make a read-aloud instructional *and* beautiful and compelling at the same time.

There are several wonderful books already in the field about the importance of reading aloud by literacy greats such as Jim Trelease (2013), Lester Laminack (2016), and Mem Fox (2001). Those books leave no doubt about the importance of reading aloud and demonstrate the instructional moves teachers can make in order to teach real reading inside one. This book is a deeper dive into the *artistry* of reading aloud. It is a user-friendly guide that builds a bridge between the artistic world and the teacher's classroom. It's a rich exploration of the way in which teaching in general, and specifically the interactive read-aloud, is as full of artistic and creative potential as any other great work of art.

How to Read This Book

When I set about writing this book, I thought about the guiding principles that have informed my approach to reading aloud to children in classrooms as well as the instructional, listening, and engaging moves I make. Ultimately, I chose ten. These principles guide my work as a teacher and an artist in general and have been inspired by many years of working in all kinds of classrooms, theatres, arts-based spaces, and learning environments. Each chapter focuses on a specific guiding principle that can deepen the impact of our interactive read-alouds. And within each chapter there are also several specific tips for incorporating the principle into your daily work with children. These concrete tips are a way of breaking down a more abstract principle so that you can try things on immediately and successfully.

While the order of these principles is intentional, you may decide not to read this book in a linear fashion. There is no exact order to thinking about these principles, so feel free to read out of order should certain ideas catch your attention first! Rather than reading the whole book at once, you may end up dipping into one or two chapters at a time and focusing specifically on only a few principles, threading those new understandings and tips into your work. There will no doubt be some ideas that *may* feel a bit uncomfortable at first, but I am sending you courage in advance for trying on a new stance and embracing a willingness to slow down and make space for words to come alive.

While these ten principles are certainly specific to the read-aloud, they extend beyond that part of the day. I hope that you learn actionable strategies and ideas for creating real moments of artistry during your interactive read-alouds but also that you consider applying these principles to other times of your day or other components of your curriculum. As you read, I hope you continue to tap into your own innate artistic impulses; approach your daily read-alouds with even more imagination, curiosity, and vision; and begin to listen or look a little differently than before. Sometimes when I read professional books, I finish reading and begin overhauling and deconstructing everything about my choices and teaching life. Rest assured—this book will not send you down that rabbit hole! This is a guide to creating greater engagement, joy, connection, and beauty in your teaching life overall.

1

Why Read-Aloud Matters

Raising a Culture of Readers

When I say that reading aloud will change the world, I know it sounds simple. But one of the many great things about giving kids access to the power of stories and sharing them together is that it is simple. It is also cheap and easily done. And the impact is huge.

—PAM ALLYN

R eading aloud to children every single day is one of the most important things any teacher can do to help children grow and become better readers, better thinkers, and, frankly, better human beings. The more I read to children in classrooms and to teachers and graduate students with whom I work, the more convinced I am that it is one of the most powerful tools we have to raise kids, teach kids, and create compassionate and civil communities. Scores of researchers and literacy advocates agree with me. A 2018 International Literacy Association leadership brief states, "Reading aloud is undoubtedly one of the most important instructional activities to help children develop the fundamental skills and knowledge needed to become readers" (2). Reading aloud was also called "the single most important activity for building the knowledge required for eventual success in reading," according to the seminal publication *Becoming a Nation of Readers* (Anderson et al. 1985, 23). One of my favorite literacy leaders, Donalyn Miller, says it best, however: "I make sure that I read to my students every day, no matter what else I cut" (2016). When I was a classroom teacher, I did the same. No matter what, I read aloud to my students every single day. And as a parent, I do too. Sometimes I send them to school without really brushing their hair, but I never skip reading aloud!

And yet, many teachers still feel they don't have enough time to read to their kids. I hear from teachers all the time about the pressures they feel to fit everything in and to make sure everything they are doing meets the standards for quality instructional time. My response to this is always the same. There is virtually nothing you could do that would be more valuable and important than reading aloud every day, not just because kids love it and are able to experience the joy and delight books can provide but also because it fuels their ability and desire to read.

Teaching children how to read is not a simple thing, and every child's reading journey is unique. There are a few things, however, that are indisputable. Children need rich and varied exposure to books and words and positive experiences with books and reading that set them on a course to become lifelong readers. Young children also need explicit instruction in the technical aspects of print, which includes instruction in phonemic awareness, spelling patterns, and phonics. While this book is obviously not intended to be a primer on how to teach children to read, there is no question that the interactive read-aloud is an essential part of any classroom's comprehensive literacy curriculum. Richard Allington (n.d.) goes so far as to suggest that 20 percent of instructional time in K–12 classrooms should be spent reading aloud.

In an *Educational Leadership* article, Allington and his colleague Gabriel (2012) lay out six elements of instruction that every child should experience every day. One of them is listening to a fluent reader read aloud. While this book is not another reiteration about *why* reading aloud is so essential, it feels important to provide a context for the ideas here.

Access

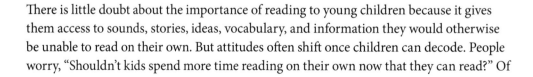

There is little doubt about the importance of reading to young children because it gives them access to sounds, stories, ideas, vocabulary, and information they would otherwise be unable to read on their own. But attitudes often shift once children can decode. People worry, "Shouldn't kids spend more time reading on their own now that they can read?" Of course, they absolutely should be reading on their own, and we should give them plenty of time to do that work at school and at home. But reading aloud remains essential.

Once children can decode, they still have plenty to do in order to become masterful readers. Reading requires doing many kinds of mental work all at the same time: decoding words, dealing with the print, thinking, imagining, envisioning, predicting, questioning, putting things together, and more. That's a lot of cognitive work for a young person. More often than I'd like to admit, I find *myself* halfway down a page, thinking, "Wait a minute. I just read all those paragraphs and I have no idea what is going on or what I just read."

When we read to children, we remove one enormous piece of the cognitive load. We take away the pressures of the print, freeing kids up to think. They can develop their thinking muscles no matter how tricky the text is. Even if they *can* read complicated text, reading to them still allows them to focus all their energy on the movie in their minds. I listen to audiobooks all the time, and sometimes it is with those books where the picture in my mind is most strong, where I can recall the actions, feelings, or voice of a character with far greater detail and nuance. This is partly because the reader is particularly expressive or masterfully captures the voice or mood of the book. Ben Berkley, the twelve-year-old son of my best friend from childhood, said it best in an email: "When I read to myself, I have to sit up and have the lights on and my brain has to be working to think about reading. When you read to me, the lights can be lower, my brain isn't so busy, and my thinking is more free" (email message to author, October 20, 2015).

Some kids have no trouble decoding words but are fooling us with their fluency. They can read all the words on a page, but they are doing something more like word calling than reading. They wouldn't be able to retell the important parts, ask thoughtful questions, or imagine the words, actions, or ideas in their brain. For kids to get better at reading, they need to read books that match their independent reading level; books they can read with both accuracy *and* comprehension. For other kids, what they can read independently doesn't match the complexity or sophistication of what they can understand, discuss, or think about. According to Jim Trelease (2013), author of the famous *Read-Aloud Handbook*, a child's reading level doesn't catch up to his listening level until eighth grade. This means teachers can give all children in their classrooms access to books that they otherwise couldn't read independently.

And what about the kids who are not able yet to do that difficult decoding work, who struggle even more significantly with the demands of print? Read-aloud is a lifeline to books and stories that would otherwise be out of reach, given the demands of the print. And I say that word in earnest: read-aloud is a *lifeline*. For all kids. But for those who struggle with reading—and there are a lot of kids who struggle for various reasons—it is often a source of frustration, discomfort, and even shame. By reading aloud to them every day, you are giving all kids access to the magic and beauty and power of story. You are giving them windows and mirrors, stories of hope, resilience, courage, and community that they otherwise might not be able to experience—in the company of one another. And you're giving every child a powerful sense of reading identity. You are saying, "Welcome to the wonderful reading club. You belong here. You are a thinker and a lover of books!"

But that's not all. By reading every day in your classroom, you are giving children access to literary conversations and to the ideas and inner worlds of one another. Engaging in daily literature conversations "provides measurable benefits in comprehension, motivation, and even language competence" (Allington and Gabriel 2012). It's almost impossible not to have literate conversations while reading aloud quality children's literature to kids. Even just asking kids to pause and tell a neighbor what they are thinking or wondering gives them practice with talking about their reading. And even short conversations and turn-and-talks during a read-aloud have an impact.

Modeling

What we model for kids is what they remember most. It is no surprise to me that my former elementary students and graduate students always remember the books we read together. Some of them even remember the books and authors I turned them on to or the books I helped them choose to read independently. I say this because the thing that mattered most to me as a teacher was modeling my fierce love of books and stories, modeling my own rich reading life, and modeling a passion for the way books can change the way we think about everything. I learned from Lucy Calkins that we absolutely must wear our love for literature, books, and words on our sleeve, that all students deserve teachers who are the mentor texts for what it means to live richly literate lives. It is critical to their literacy development. And most of the time, my students left my classroom with a hunger and an appetite for books, with an abiding sense that great books are among the great wonders of the world.

Reading aloud is the most effective way to model for students what real reading looks and sounds like. How else can we show students what the invisible processes of reading and thinking look like? How else can students hear what it sounds like to read fluently, expressively, and in a way that allows you to really see and understand what's happening? How can we model the love we have for books unless we actually show kids our genuine reactions, enthusiasm, and experience of reading real books? I think it's safe to say that most teachers got into teaching because they wanted to help raise a generation of kids who would be lifetime readers, not just schooltime readers who only read because it was an assignment. Obviously, if you're reading this book, you agree that the reason we get good at reading is not to score well on standardized tests. Knowing how essential reading aloud is for students of all ages helps us justify our daily read-aloud practice to folks who might not otherwise know what's best for kids *and* push back against the narrative that scoring well on tests is the purpose of our teaching.

Even if we just read aloud without pausing to think aloud or prompt kids to think, envision, or talk, that alone would be powerful modeling. Listening to a fluent, expressive reader helps kids understand that *that* is how reading is supposed to go in their minds! And a teacher who models her love and amazement while reading sends a powerful message: this is how fabulous book reading can be.

But interactive read-alouds also make it possible to explicitly model comprehension skills that powerful readers need to utilize in order to gain real understanding. By thinking aloud, we are modeling the way we put together the threads of a book, think carefully about characters, and get the picture clear in our minds. By voicing our confusion about a word or complicated part, we are explicitly demonstrating what proficient readers do when they encounter trouble. By modeling the whole host of comprehension strategies strong readers use as they move through a text, we are modeling authentically—in the context of a real book, not a prefabricated passage that is designed for the practice of strategies in isolation. The modeling that occurs in the context of reading aloud demonstrates an orchestration of strategies that readers use on the fly, all at once, as we read. When we read books, we don't decide to *only* envision, predict, or infer. Conductors don't conduct one instrument at a time—just the oboe or just the clarinet. When reading aloud, we actively employ the whole gamut of comprehension skills; we model the whole orchestra.

To be sure, we can overmodel as well. See Chapter 12, "Choose Wisely," for more on the balance between letting the words and the story do their work and modeling explicit thinking and comprehension strategies effectively. Students will sometimes say, "Just read!" (as do my own kids!) when I start bogging down the read-aloud experience with too many interruptions. It is a fine balance! But we can't forgo the opportunity to open up our brains so children can witness the inner workings of a strong reader in action.

There is another, equally important, kind of modeling that reading aloud affords, especially for big kids who are beginning to face bigger decisions and challenges—the modeling of compassion, kindness, and openheartedness. Contemporary children's and young adult literature tackles issues that children are facing today: the effects of intolerance, bullying, and racism, as well as war, displacement, and other humanitarian crises. We are in an ever-changing world with ever-expanding and overwhelming access to information. Our children must learn to navigate the pull of various screens and devices. Reading a book together with a group of children makes it possible to quiet and focus our screen-obsessed brains, to gather together around a story that shines a light on any number of big issues, and to show up for one another. When we go on a journey with a character who's navigating tough situations that many of our kids are facing, we are able to give space for honest discussion and model careful listening. We can model compassion not only for the characters in the stories but for one another. Reading aloud can help make our classrooms kinder, more generous places, which provide a model for the kind of world we are all trying to create.

Joy

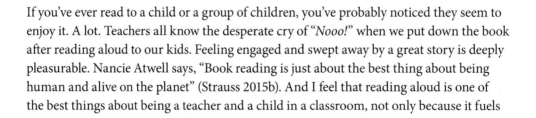

If you've ever read to a child or a group of children, you've probably noticed they seem to enjoy it. A lot. Teachers all know the desperate cry of *Nooo!* when we put down the book after reading aloud to our kids. Feeling engaged and swept away by a great story is deeply pleasurable. Nancie Atwell says, "Book reading is just about the best thing about being human and alive on the planet" (Strauss 2015b). And I feel that reading aloud is one of the best things about being a teacher and a child in a classroom, not only because it fuels kids' reading lives but because it fills kids (and teachers!) up with joy. And that is not to be underestimated.

Joy is serious business. I think we should be talking more about the importance of joy in our classrooms. Quite simply, we are more productive, more engaged, and more open to learning when we are happy. Lots of serious folks in the world of business are looking closely at the role of happiness at work and the impact it has on the bottom line. From Shawn Achor's international best-seller *The Happiness Advantage: How a Positive Brain Fuels Success in Work and Life* (2018), to studies on the benefits of happy people at work conducted by management consulting firms, to happiness-at-work-themed TED talks that have been viewed millions of times, the field of positive psychology is on fire. It isn't too far a leap to wonder about the role of happiness at school and the impact it has on students.

So, where does read-aloud fit in to all this? In the simplest terms, read-aloud makes kids happy. It's a surefire way to create moments of joy at school, which creates the conditions for kids to do their best learning.

And reading aloud is one of the most effective strategies available for addressing what Kelly Gallagher (2009) calls *readicide*, which he defines as "the systematic killing of the love of reading" (2) and which occurs, according to Steven Wolk (2010), when the only kind of reading we ask kids to do in schools seems "designed to make reading painful, tedious, and irrelevant" (10).

If kids don't experience the joy in reading, how can we expect them to see the point? If the bulk of their experiences with reading are painful or tedious, how will they grow into lifelong readers? Creating joyful learning and reading experiences is not fluff because kids who love to read, read more. And kids who read more do better in school and (because it's a reality we have to face . . .) do better on tests.

Throughout the process of writing this book, I spent time in lots of classrooms, reading to different communities of kids and focusing on different aspects of this work. But one thing struck me in particular: how much the older kids, and even the adults, were affected by the experience of listening. Time after time when I read to middle school classrooms, they wondered aloud when I might come back to keep reading the book we had started together. "Do you like when teachers read aloud to you?" I inquired, and kids confirmed that they really did but that it didn't happen much anymore; it stopped in third or fourth grade, and they missed it. Librarian Mary Zdrojewski found this to be true as well, when she began working with teenagers in her New York school district. When she asked students what they wanted from their library class, she expected to hear requests for coding, robotics, or hands-on projects. But, she said, "they just wanted [her] to read aloud to them" (Vercelletto 2018).

I wasn't surprised by that story. Most of my work is with adults, with teachers who have just started their practice and teachers who are forty-year veterans. I almost always start a day with reading aloud, by filling the space with words, with story, with an experience that unites and connects us all. And just like when I read to kids, something shifts in the room, something cracks open between all of us. And when I ask the teachers the same question I ask the kids, "Did you enjoy that experience?" the answers are almost always the same: "Yes," they say, "it has been a long time since someone read to us like that. We forgot how much we loved it." Friends of mine who are parenting teenagers find this to be true as well: reading a book aloud with their middle and high schoolers creates a space for connection and conversation with their kids during what is often a tricky time of life. Recently, when I returned to a school to lead professional development, the principal told me she started reading Sharon Draper's *Out of My Mind* to her eleven- and thirteen-year-old sons after my previous workshop. "As we read the book together," she told me, "I could feel my older son's love for reading return. It was so refreshing to read together again, and I was so surprised by their full engagement. It's the best book club I belong to!"

We don't age out of the read-aloud experience. Reading to kids is a vital part of creating a community of readers in your classroom and supporting a balanced, rigorous, and joyful literacy curriculum that feeds your students' souls and minds as well as your own.

2

Teachers as Creative Artists

Tapping into Our Curiosity

For students who know reading as a personal art, every day is a transfusion. Every day they engage with literature that enables them to know things, feel things, imagine things, hope for things, *become people* they never could have dreamed without the transforming power of books, books, books.

—NANCY ATWELL

My greatest wish as an educator is that young people come to see reading as a "personal art," as a means of personal transformation, and as a gateway to the world within and the world all around. If reading is a personal art, then perhaps the interactive read-aloud is a *classroom* art, a creative process that centers children's literature as powerful works of art in their own right, with the potential to instruct, inspire, disrupt, heal, and empower.

Literacy teachers are responsible for teaching all the components of proficient reading and writing. That is a big job, and sometimes we become bogged down by the demands of assessment, accountability, differentiation, and instructional mandates against the backdrop of limited time and resources. This book is not an antidote to any of that, but it is an invitation to see ourselves not just as literacy teachers but also as creative artists who engage children in perhaps the most important artistic medium of all: reading.

Being a great teacher demands an extraordinary amount of creativity. And although a read-aloud is not a performance—which might suggest something showy or artificial—it can and should have elements of artistry. I recently saw the moving and hilarious play *A Funny Thing Happened on the Way to the Gynecologic Oncology Unit at Memorial Sloan Kettering Cancer Center of New York City*. Halley Feiffer, the playwright and main character in the piece, wrote this in the playbill:

> *I don't know if I ever feel more present than when I'm in a theatre watching a play—or acting in a play—because it's a group of people who are are all setting the intention to be present and focus on a living, breathing, changing experience at the same time. You're forced to be utterly present and available and to surrender. You're telling a story and subsuming your own needs and wants and desire for the sake of the story and it's very, very hard. It's like creating a Tibetan sand mandala where it's impossible to get it perfect, but you do your best, and then it's gone. It's absolutely thrilling and it's the most pure form of art that I know how to engage in. Also, it's just really really fun. (Levinson 2017)*

When I read those lines, I stopped in my tracks. I could easily substitute "classroom" for "theatre" and "reading aloud" for "watching a play." The meaning would stay the same. Our students are yearning for opportunities to engage with stories and books in ways that are artistic and pure, that will give them the chance to be a part of a *living, breathing, changing experience* as a community, that will allow them to think and imagine, talk and connect, and live inside a text in authentic, meaningful ways.

If we are to help children see that book reading is, as Nancie Atwell says, "just about the best thing about being human and alive on the planet" (Strauss 2015b), however, we have our work cut out for us. There's some serious competition out there for our students' attention, so it is incumbent upon us to make books come alive in our rooms by tapping into the creative potential inherent inside any read-aloud. Full disclosure: I identify as an artist, and for a time even, I made a (meager!) living as an actress and a singer, so I might feel more immediately comfortable employing some of the artistic principles laid out in this book. But creativity is not for the few.

Elizabeth Gilbert defines creative living as "choosing the path of curiosity over the path of fear" (2016) and challenges the idea that creativity is for the gifted or the special. "Every human child is born doing this stuff innately," she says. "It's an instinct. There's no child that you put crayons and paper in front of who doesn't get it, what you're supposed to do" (2016). As teachers we are constantly called to be curious—about a child, the dynamics of our classroom, a lesson plan, and so on. Our curiosity propels us to ask better questions, notice with more depth and insight, and reflect with more wisdom. It keeps us fresh and alive, present and joyful in the classroom, and it fuels our creativity. Every year we have new students to get curious about, and every single day children are changing and growing into new people. We are always inventing solutions to wide-ranging problems. This is all to say that each of us has the right to claim our creative selves, knowing that our curiosity and creativity fuel not only our read-alouds but our teaching, our relationships with kids, and our interactions all day long.

Naomi Shihab Nye tells one of my favorite stories about the power of both read-aloud and creative thinking. During a school visit, she was struck by how much the students loved poetry and thought to herself, "Wow. I don't know what's going on in this school" (2016). She had forgotten about a conversation she'd had with the principal a few years back about poetry, where he'd talked about how much he had always loved poetry but couldn't really use it because he was "just a principal." Nye had been undeterred and asked whether or not he had an intercom, which of course he had. "Well, why don't you read a poem to start off the day for the entire school?" she had suggested. It turned out he had done just that. One of the students told her, "Our principal reads us a poem. And so we carry poems with us every day. We have them in our heads."

Our questions and curiosity can lead us to creative solutions, especially around our commitment to deep engagement with reading. Like that principal, we might wonder, "How do we inspire kids to love poetry?" Or we might ask any of the following questions.

- How can we create more engaging experiences with books or make this particular book come alive?
- Why are these books not reaching my students and what else might be out there?
- How can we be the kind of school community that puts our love of words and literature front and center?
- What book would this particular kid love or even need to read?
- How can we model the power of words and reading for as many kids as possible?

- How can we create a true culture of reading at our school?
- How can our instruction amplify student voices?

The answers might be as simple as an intercom or as visionary as World Read Aloud Day, dreamed up by Pam Allyn's LitWorld organization. But it starts with asking the questions and getting curious about our teaching, our kids, and our communities.

In order for children to see reading as a personal art, we must give them access to the *beauty* of books even as they are learning and applying foundational skills. We should not withhold the experience of reading and thinking imaginatively until children have mastered decoding or successfully demonstrated their ability to determine the main idea of a piece of text. Sir Ken Robinson reminds us:

> *Creativity is not a linear process, in which you have to learn all the necessary skills before you get started. It is true that creative work in any field involves a growing mastery of skills and concepts. It is not true that they have to be mastered before the creative work can begin. Focusing on skills in isolation can kill interest in any discipline. Many people have been put off mathematics for life by endless rote tasks that did nothing to inspire them with the beauty of numbers. Many have spent years grudgingly practicing scales for music examinations only to abandon the instrument altogether once they've made the grade. (Robinson and Aronica 2015, 120)*

No matter where we teach, no matter whom we teach, the interactive read-aloud is an effective and available tool for teaching real reading, but also creative, collaborative, and critical thinking. Fortunately, it does not require any special gadgets or technology, advanced training, or financial resources. We can all do it well, and we can all help students tap into their own creativity and imagination as a result.

So the question remains, how do we actually make our teaching, and specifically our read-alouds, more artful? While it is impossible to distill what exactly makes an artistic process successful, this book makes the connection between artistic endeavors and the art of reading aloud, laying out ten principles that teachers can use to make their read-alouds rich with engagement, instruction, connection, and purpose. In any read-aloud, I am not thinking about activating any one principle at any given time; these principles fuel a creative stance—they thread through and elevate my teaching of reading (and other subjects) in general.

Ten Principles of the Artful Read-Aloud

1. EMBODY THE TEXT.

2. MAKE MEANING.

3. STAY OPEN.

4. LOOK UP.

5. INVITE CONVERSATION.

6. TAKE A BREATH.

7. BE AWED.

8. DIG DEEP.

9. MOVE AROUND.

10. CHOOSE WISELY.

My work as a literacy educator is informed by a wide range of experiences and collaborations with districts, schools, classrooms, colleagues, kids, artists, arts-based organizations, literacy-based organizations, nonprofits, and think tanks, all of which I cite throughout the book. One specific framework, however, has informed my thinking for years as I've developed links between the teaching of reading, and specifically the interactive read-aloud, and creativity. The Ten Capacities for Imaginative Learning, which anchor Lincoln Center Education's approach to arts education, resonate throughout this book:

1. **Notice deeply.** *How many layers of detail can you identify if you take the time? Can you go deeper?* Noticing deeply is at the heart of every chapter in this book. Each artistic principle is informed by paying close attention—not just to the words or illustrations on the page but to the students in front of you; your own thinking, choices, and emotional responses; and the experience you are helping to shape in the room.

2. **Embody.** *Use your body to explore your ideas and to experience a work of art through your senses. Try it out.* The principles *embody the text* and *move around* are directly linked to this concept, but so too are *look up*, *take a breath*, and *be awed*, all of which discuss the way in which reading aloud makes deep emotional connection possible.

3. **Pose questions.** *What do you wonder?* The principles *make meaning, dig deep, stay open*, and *invite conversation* all address the importance of asking questions and staying open to continued learning between students and also from students. This capacity informs my work when I am teaching students to wonder, but it also reminds me to stay curious whenever I am teaching and learning.

4. **Make connections.** *How is this like something else? Make personal, textual, and wider connections.* As we read aloud, we make it possible for students to have a rich and deeply engaging experience around text that informs their future reading. Our read-alouds create a shared literary and artistic experience that can be connected to their independent reading throughout the school year, in our conferences and small-group work.

5. **Identify patterns.** *How might different details relate? Analyze them.* The principles *be awed, make meaning*, and *dig deep* value the importance of looking carefully at the details in text through rereading and close reading of the text, the illustrations, an author's word choice, and an illustrator's artistic choices.

6. **Empathize.** *Can you understand how others think and feel? What are their perspectives?* This is another principle that threads across chapters. I can think of nothing else that helps children build community and experience the humanity of one another (and the characters whom they grow to know) as well as the interactive read-aloud.

7. **Live with ambiguity.** *What if there is not just one answer? Be patient with ambiguity.* In a sense, living with ambiguity is part of what makes reading complicated text so challenging, but it is also what I love most about being a reader. Life will always be full of ambiguities and complexities, but book reading creates a quiet space in our brains for contemplating multiple points of view and managing uncertainty, especially as many books do not have tidy endings or circumstances. Modeling how readers navigate complex text, hold onto their questions, and develop and revise their thinking is also one of the most important functions of reading aloud. This idea also relates to our own approach as teachers learning to live with ambiguity as we invite kids into conversation, stay open to their ideas and thinking, and make meaning alongside and in front of them during our read-alouds. Living with ambiguity is a capacity that threads through several of my principles: *stay open*, *make meaning*, *invite conversation*, *dig deep*, and *choose wisely*.

8. **Create meaning.** *Bring together what you've thought so far. What new interpretations can you make? See these new interpretations in the light of others in the community and express it in in your own voice.* This is at the heart of reading aloud—to make meaning in the company of others. The role of the teacher is part facilitator, part reading expert–in-residence, and part artistic collaborator, whose goal is to help students listen and learn from each other and develop ideas in partnership and on their own.

9. **Take action.** *What will you choose to do with your ideas? Put them into practice.* While *move around* and *dig deep* are the most obvious principles that connect to this capacity, the read-aloud energizes students to take action as readers. Students' desire to take on a more rigorous reading life and their ability to view themselves as thinkers and meaning makers and to see the

purpose and delight of books are directly linked to the work we do during the interactive read-aloud.

10. **Reflect and assess.** *Look back on what you've experienced. What have you learned? What's next?* We are constantly reflecting and assessing as we read aloud to students. Listening in to their talk, looking over their jots or written responses, even paying attention to their body language and engagement all inform our future instruction. When we read aloud we are creating opportunities to reflect as teachers and giving students opportunities to pause and reflect within themselves, with a partner or small group, or with writing.

In her book *Big Magic*, Elizabeth Gilbert writes "we are all walking repositories of buried treasures. The hunt to uncover these jewels—that's creative living" (2015, 8). I believe we can hunt for buried treasure inside the books we read aloud, bringing forth their magic. More importantly, however, is the process of hunting for jewels *in community* with your students, reading books together that uncover the magic of all of our imaginations. When we read artfully, we make it practically impossible for students not to fall in love with books and begin to know reading as a personal art themselves. We help students see themselves as readers and see one another as fellow story lovers and human beings who are gathered together to listen, to learn, and to understand the world and all its treasure trove of great characters, big ideas, new information, and life-changing stories a little better.

3

Principle One

Embody the Text

Helping students see books come to life

Dancing is music made visible.

—GEORGE BALANCHINE

When we read on our own, we don't tend to act out what we are seeing, learning about, or experiencing. That would be quite a sight, wouldn't it? The truth is, however, when we read with deep comprehension, we can feel as though we are transported into the story—racing through the forest, reuniting with a loved one, or reaching out our hands to say hello. Or when we read an informational text, we imagine the texture of an animal's skin or feel the heat of a volcanic eruption. In our minds, we are often having a fully activated sensory experience, even though we are sitting quietly in reading nooks or our classrooms.

When children are just starting to read on their own, we often teach and reinforce the idea that reading should feel like watching a "movie in our minds" (Calkins and Tolan 2015, 81). Essentially, we are teaching kids to envision as they read—one of the key comprehension skills of strong readers. The reason we often feel we have traveled back in time or have met and befriended new people in the pages of a book is directly linked to the movie we have been silently watching in our minds the whole time. Those images we construct are often highly specific. I can still imagine Opal's face when she opens the door to her trailer, hoping to convince her father to keep Winn-Dixie. In my mind, she pushes open the door carefully and tentatively. Her eyes are filled with hopeful yearning, but there is a look of worry in them as well. Before she starts to speak, she takes a breath. None of this is in the book, by the way, but it's what I see in my mind when I read (and remember) those pages.

When we read aloud, we have an opportunity to bring to life the words on the page and demonstrate the reader's envisioning mind. In a sense, we are doing a version of what George Balanchine describes in the epigraph: embodying the text is *reading made visible*. The metaphor "watching a movie in your mind," while useful, doesn't fully capture what it *feels like* to be transported in a book. When we read with deep comprehension and engagement, there is a sense that our whole selves are inside the text, that our bodies as well as our minds are actively involved.

Embodying the text as we read aloud can involve simple gestures and movements, but it is transformative for kids watching and listening. And while we don't have to go to the great lengths that performers do when they embody their roles onstage, there are elements of their work that teachers can borrow in order to elevate the power of our classroom read-alouds.

I am particularly struck by the way solo performers—actors who perform an entire show on their own—are able to embody multiple characters through distinct shifts in voice, movement, and physicality. When you watch a truly great solo artist, like Nilaja Sun, Anna Deveare Smith, or Sarah Jones, it is astonishing to see them move in and out of character seamlessly. You sometimes forget you are watching only one person!

James Lecesne is another such artist. The *New York Times* calls him "one of the most talented solo performers of his (or any) generation" (Isherwood 2015), and after seeing his solo show, *The Absolute Brightness of Leonard Pelkey*, at the Old Globe Theatre in San Diego, I was not surprised. The play tells the funny, heartbreaking story of a missing teenager in a small New Jersey town, and Lecesne embodies a huge range of characters, including the woman who runs the local beauty parlor and the lead detective on the case. In a note inside the playbill, the artistic director of the theatre, Barry Edelstein, said this about the art of solo performing:

> *The solo performance brings us back to the ancient roots of theater art, to the purest impulse of storytelling, to the iconic, eternal image of an intimate tale told around a campfire. Just words, just the human voice, its listeners transfixed. At*

the same time, the solo performer comes as close as anything in the theater to daredevilry. What could be braver? One talented actor, armed only with his or her voice, body, and imagination, ventures onto the stage and weaves a spell that captivates an audience for an evening. Part stand-up comic, part shaman, the solo performer conjures an entire world from the resources within. (2017)

Did you think the same thing I did when you read that? Did you think, "He's describing teachers!"? What we do every day comes as close to daredevilry as anything in this world. And managing, inspiring, and teaching a large group of children—you'd better believe that requires an entire world of resources within. Part stand-up comic, part shaman indeed! The work of the solo artist, who leaves listeners transfixed, is the work of the teacher during read-aloud. So what specifically can we learn from these spectacular artists who use only their voices, bodies, and imagination to bring an entire story to life?

Tip 1: First, Find the Voices

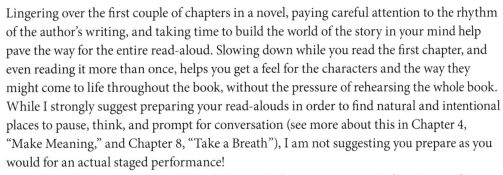

Lingering over the first couple of chapters in a novel, paying careful attention to the rhythm of the author's writing, and taking time to build the world of the story in your mind help pave the way for the entire read-aloud. Slowing down while you read the first chapter, and even reading it more than once, helps you get a feel for the characters and the way they might come to life throughout the book, without the pressure of rehearsing the whole book. While I strongly suggest preparing your read-alouds in order to find natural and intentional places to pause, think, and prompt for conversation (see more about this in Chapter 4, "Make Meaning," and Chapter 8, "Take a Breath"), I am not suggesting you prepare as you would for an actual staged performance!

When I read a book aloud, I don't have a single narrator voice. I adjust it according to the text, the narrator telling the story, and the tone of the book. Sometimes my voice is light and high-pitched. Sometimes the character is more tentative, and my voice slows down. When I read to primary-age kids, the stories are often about or told by younger children, which means I can be sillier and lighter with my voice. But with older students, I find my voice often drops down and has a more straightforward, serious tone. The most important first step, however, is to try to hear the voices of the narrator and the main characters in the book in order to get a sense of who they are. In order to begin developing his characters, James Lecesne says he does something similar: "I hear them speaking and then I work back" (Kachka 2015).

Sometimes finding the voice of the narrator means thinking mostly about one character telling the story throughout the book. In other books, however, there are several voices to consider right away. In *The Vanderbeekers of 141st Street* (Glaser 2017), we are introduced to all seven characters in this wonderful, bighearted family right away. In the opening scene, the Vanderbeeker parents have convened their children for a family meeting in order to tell them their landlord is refusing to renew their lease, but before they can share that information, the kids begin throwing out their own ideas for what the big news could be.

"Right-o," said Papa. "Good news first." He paused and adjusted his glasses. "You kids all know how much Mama and I love you, right?"

I hear a forced jauntiness in Papa, which is fun to embody.

Oliver, who was nine years old and wise to the ways of the world, put down his book and squinted. "Are you guys getting divorced? Jimmy L's parents got a divorce. Then they let him get a pet snake." He kicked the backs of his sneakers against the tall stack of ancient encyclopedias he was sitting on.

I love how Oliver blurts out the question of whether or not they are getting a divorce and then matter-of-factly mentions his friend's parents' divorce and resulting pet snake. There's something hilariously nonplussed about him.

"No, we're—" Papa began.

"Is it true?" six-year-old Hyacinth whispered, tears pooling in her round eyes.

"Of course we're—" Mama said.

I hear Hyacinth's voice much like my own little six-year-old daughter's—high pitched, breathy with emotion, and near tears as she asks this question.

"What's a dorce?" interrupted Laney, who was four and three-quarters years old and practicing her forward rolls on the carpet. She was wearing an outfit of red plaids, lavender stripes, and aqua polka dots that she had matched herself.

Little Laney's voice sounds earnest, wide-eyed, and innocent.

"It means Mama and Papa don't love each other anymore," said twelve-year-old Jessie, glaring at her parents from behind chunky black eyeglasses. "What a nightmare."

Can't you just imagine the twelve-year-old Jessie's indignation toward her parents and the simultaneous eye roll as she says this?

"We'll have to split our time between them," added Isa, Jessie's twin. She was holding her violin, and jabbed her bow against the arm of the couch. "Alternating holidays and summers and whatnot. I think I'm going to be sick."

And Isa's irritation and outrage. It's like she spits out the words about being sick.

Mama threw up her hands. "STOP! Just . . . everyone, please. Stop." . . . Mama glanced at Papa, took a deep breath, and briefly closed her eyes. (2–3)

I confess, I hear myself in Mama—exasperated but keeping it together and taking control!

When I read that little scene, right away I begin hearing and bringing this family to life in my mind, which is a crucial first step anytime we take a journey through a book. When you get started in a new book, take a minute to linger over the first series of scenes where characters are introduced. Think about how the characters' voices might sound, which in turn will inform your overall understanding for what kind of people they might be, how they might move in the world, and even what is going on for them internally.

Considering how you *hear* the voices has an impact on the way in which you *use* your voice while you read aloud. And it helps you teach into the important work students need to do when they read on their own, which is to differentiate between the voices, hear them clearly, and really imagine them as they read. After reading aloud from *The Vanderbeekers*, you could pull a small group together or teach a minilesson that made your process explicit, so kids could remember to take a moment to linger over the voices in their books as well, to get curious about how their characters might sound and subsequently what that might reveal about who they are.

For a very different sort of book, like *Rules* (Lord 2006), the work of the first chapter is finding the voice of twelve-year-old Catherine (who narrates the whole story), but it's also figuring out how to give voice to her younger brother, David, who is on the autism spectrum. I read *Rules* aloud almost every year as a fourth-grade teacher. For this book, I felt I had to tread carefully with some of the voices. For one, it's important to respectfully honor the voice of David without taking it too far. And that is true whenever I take on the voice of someone dissimilar to me. I am careful not to overplay it. I don't want my voice to sound like a caricature and I don't want to sound like I am making a joke. When scenes are emotional, I allow my voice to match that emotion, but I am careful to be tuned in to the *emotion* without necessarily overdramatizing a character's voice or personality. I read books that feature characters who are outside my own cultural background and experience (a different race, ethnicity, or nationality) a lot. I recognize that there are lines or characters who most likely don't sound like me, but I read those lines and characters anyway, without exaggeration and absolutely without any superfluous accents.

In order for kids to experience the stories of lots of different people, in order to make sure all kids can see and hear themselves in print, I am mindful that I am often reading stories that are not my own, especially as a white middle-class woman. And that can sometimes be uncomfortable. But we must give kids access to books that tell all kinds of important stories: about injustice, disability, unlikely friendships, racial tension, and more. When I sense that I might be delving into uncomfortable territory, I simply lean on the words, letting them do the work for me. I don't comment on them. I just read them, clearly and plainly as they are written. It's not simple, and yet it is. It's not simple to inhabit the lives and experiences of other people, to give voice to the stories of characters who are worlds away from me—both literally and figuratively. So I simply read the words and get out of their way.

I thought about this a lot as I read aloud Jewell Parker Rhodes' stunning book *Ghost Boys* (2018). I was spending time in middle school classrooms in San Diego, working on creating a robust culture around reading, and *Ghost Boys* was one of those books that utterly captured the attention of every sixth-, seventh-, and eighth-grade room I visited. *Ghost Boys* moves between sections titled "Alive" and "Dead" and tells the story of twelve-year-old Jerome, who is killed by a policeman but is able to witness events going on around him after his death. This is a harrowing book and it's painful to read and inhabit. One reason I felt empowered to read it aloud, and in front of so many fellow teachers and administrators, was because of something its author had said at a conference I attended shortly before I started using it in the classroom, which is to remember that the book and teachers are partners! Together with the words of the book, we can give kids access to important stories; we can speak aloud the words of characters in a book, knowing that the author wanted those words and characters to come alive in the imaginations of students. We can honor these stories and the characters telling them with our own voices, even if our voices might not sound exactly like the ones written into the story.

Tip 2: Next, Find the Physicality

The next step is to consider how characters might move through the world, or how you might physicalize the concepts being taught. For some books, I rely more heavily on voice, but for others the small physical shifts I make as I read help students envision characters and action more fully. Please note the word *small*; I am not recommending that you stand up to do full-blown performances. Not only would many of us balk at that idea, but it also doesn't square with what this time of day is about: creating authentic and artful reading experiences that also fuel children's reading lives. The artfulness is in service of the learning and the literature.

Video 1
Bringing
Characters and
Actions to Life

See p. ix on how to
access this video
clip and others
found in the book.

But we can learn from solo artists who are in the business of creating fully realized characters for the stage. In a *New York Magazine* article, James Lecesne discusses the way he is able to embody so many different characters in a span of a seventy-five-minute show (Kachka 2015). For each one, he walks and sits and stands differently, he holds his hands and tilts his head differently, and of course he alters the expressions on his face.

One of the books that I find impossible not to physicalize is *The One and Only Ivan* (Applegate 2012). Ivan, a mighty silverback gorilla, narrates the story. It can be difficult to keep track of who is who because there aren't always dialogue tags to indicate who is speaking. When I read this story aloud, I find myself using specific gestures to shift between each character. Kids (and teachers!) respond that this allows them to see more than they otherwise would have. "I could really imagine all the different characters," they say. Or, "I forgot I was listening to a book—the story really came alive!" This work also gives students a richer, more engaging experience of the book. Watch Video 1 for some examples.

Even if you don't consistently physicalize every character, the quality of your read-aloud and the voices you use as you read will no doubt be influenced by your embodiment work. Thinking about the physicality of characters will help you bring them to life with more authority. You'll have a stronger sense for how characters might move through the world, what their stance or posture could be, how they might hold their heads—upright, with confidence or certainty, or with a slight, defensive tilt. Ultimately, you will feel more connected to the characters, which will have a powerful trickle-down effect for your students; they will feel more connected and engaged as well.

Tip 3: Act It Out

Fiction: Do What the Character Is Doing

In a way, Tip 3 is the simplest, most accessible tip of all. If a character reaches into his back pocket or looks at her palm, do that exact thing as you read. When Grandma in *Those Shoes* (Boelts 2009) turns over "those shoes" in order to check the price, I turn over my hand too.

When she sees the prices and "sits down heavy," I slump in my seat. And when Grandma shakes her head, I shake mine.

> *Grandma turns those shoes over so she can check the price. When she sees it, she sits down heavy. "Maybe they wrote it down wrong," I say. Grandma shakes her head.*

At the end of the story, when Antonio leans forward to thank Jeremy for giving him his pair of too-small "those shoes," I lean forward too.

> *Standing in line to go to recess, Antonio leans forward and says, "Thanks." I smile and give him a nudge. . . . "Let's race!"*

It's important to point out that I don't mime the whole story, but these two moments—when Grandma sits down heavy and when Antonio leans forward—are significant. They are drawn out and told bit by bit (something you may want to look at again during your writing block!), which indicates that they require emphasis. So I slow down my reading and layer it with the accompanying gestures.

The opening lines of *The Magician's Elephant* describe Peter, who has "a hat on his head and a coin in his hand" (DiCamillo 2011a, 1). When Peter looks at the florit, I look at the florit. When he takes the soldier's hat off his head and puts it back on again, I gesture as though I am taking off my hat and putting it back on, not with a great flourish but with a simple gesture, in order to demonstrate just how flummoxed Peter is. This subtle gesture helps me embody Peter's consternation and confusion about what he should do in this moment. The embodiment signals to kids that they should be seeing all this in their minds and also that they should be thinking—about what kind of character Peter is and what those small actions say about his situation and the pressures he feels to please Vilna Lutz, his guardian. There are endless examples, but characters *do* things in books. And we can do them too, in order to bring a book to life with more specificity.

Nonfiction: Do What the Concept Is Explaining

Embodying the text is also an important way to help kids learn new vocabulary and concepts in nonfiction books. It is very similar to embodying the text in a fiction book, but instead of doing what characters do, you are demonstrating the descriptors and action

words that teach about a concept. When you embody a word, you scaffold meaning for that word, which is helpful for all children, but especially for English language learners, who need more visual supports to build their vocabulary. Certainly, this is an easy transfer when we read about nonfiction topics like animals, which is common in younger grades. Showing how animals get food, move around their habitat, and use their bodies is similar to embodying a character's actions or expressions. But demonstrating how you make mental models with more complicated nonfiction text helps kids understand the meaning making they should be doing when they tackle unfamiliar and difficult concepts.

Full disclosure: I am a much more voracious fiction reader than I am a nonfiction or informational one, and reading nonfiction is far more challenging for me. This is often true for kids as well, which is all the more reason to embody nonfiction text in order to help them envision and understand the information and to remind them that mental models are essential for deep comprehension. I often use articles from newspapers to show this work in action, which might seem like an unlikely source. A wonderful example is the *New York Times* article "'Lifeboats' Amid the World's Wildfires," which examines the effects of wildfires and the phenomenon of "refugia," which are described as islands of greenery that survive even the worst fires (Zimmer 2018). As I read this article, I embody the mental models I am creating in order to bring to life all this new information. Let's take a look at this tiny chunk of text:

> *The fires left scenes of ashen destruction, but they did not wipe out everything. Scattered about the ravaged landscapes were islands of trees, shrubs and grass that survived unharmed.*

As I read that, I make a scattering motion with the fingers of one hand and then I say, "Before I go on, I am pausing to make sure I can really see those different islands of green—with trees and plants—*scattered* in the midst of a destroyed forest." As I continue to read, I try to embody as much of the text as possible to help kids imagine it in their mind, pausing to demonstrate the envisioning work I am doing in my own mind.

I can also use gesture to demonstrate the way in which I'm processing the structure of the text. For example, in this article there is a difference between the kinds of refugia that are consistently able to survive wildfires and those that are fleeting. To show the way my brain organizes that information, I gesture with one hand when I read about the enduring refugia and shift to my other hand when I read about the refugia that survive only one fire.

Obviously, I can create graphic organizers that model this thinking, such as a quick T-chart, but I also want to show kids that I organize and filter information through my brain as I go.

Making the read-aloud experience more engaging and vivid to watch isn't the sole reason to embody the text. When you embody actions and descriptors throughout a reading, you are giving a subtle and consistent reminder to students that reading brains are constantly making pictures, seeing the plot in motion, living inside the story, and trying to make mental models. *All the time.*

4

Principle Two

Make Meaning

Revealing your reader brain at work

You have to have an ability to hear rhythm and to know how to place an emphasis in a string of words, so the meaning comes through.

—HARRIET WALTER, VETERAN BRITISH ACTRESS

When a teacher reads aloud, it is an opportunity to bring to life a whole world. This is the province of artists as well. The job of an actor, musician, or dancer is to bring to life the words on the page, the notes on the staff, or the story inside the music. It isn't enough to just play the notes or say the words out loud. An artist performs with a deep understanding of what each step represents, of the subtext of the words in the script, or of the shifting dynamics of a musical passage. An artist has thought deeply too about the intentions of the playwright, the composer, or the choreographer. Renowned cellist Yo-Yo Ma describes playing an instrument as "pure engineering" but says that "music happens between the notes" (Ma 2014). He describes merging the playing of the instrument (the engineering) with "the mental process, the emotional process, the psychic investment." I hear Yo-Yo Ma describing exactly what we do when we read aloud, which is to combine the pure engineering of reading with making meaning.

A teacher's fluent reading demonstrates how an expert reader makes sense of the words and understands how they should sound in one's brain, but teachers also can demonstrate for students what true meaning making sounds and looks like. We rarely have access to this when we watch an artist onstage. Can you imagine if an actor stopped in the middle of a scene, turned to the audience, and said, "So, this moment here was especially difficult to figure out. As Othello, I feel deeply suspicious of my wife but still very much in love with her. So that's why I say the line this way and react this way. . . ."?

I've seen a lot of theatre, and that's never happened—not in the middle of a show anyway. Every now and then, actors come back out onstage for talk backs, and audience members can ask them about their roles and their process. In those moments, we get a front-row seat to the thinking work that went into understanding the script, making sense of the words and the playwright's intentions, and bringing it to life. But that does not happen in the midst of the actual experience. When we read to kids, however, we can give them a front-row seat into the work an expert reader's brain does in order to understand a book, make sense of the words and the author's intentions, and bring it to life in real time!

This is why reading aloud is one of the most powerful ways to teach reading. We create authentic moments every day where students observe an expert reader's mind at work, which gives them a model for what real reading work and real thinking work actually is. Instead of asking kids to practice a comprehension skill in isolation or talk about what a skill is, we demonstrate it for them in a meaningful context. Jeffrey Wilhelm, Distinguished Professor at Boise State University and director of the Boise State Writing Project, discusses the importance of modeling expertise for kids:

> *In my own teaching life, I'm not going for proficiency; I aim to be expert. Experts possess rich mental models of their tasks, they have expert strategies for completing them, and they use these models and strategies to create new kinds of knowledge and ways of doing things. . . . [E]xperts know why they're doing something, they know how they're doing it, and they can monitor and self-correct that practice. They can justify their understanding, and they can enact it and explain it to others. . . . There is a very elegant idea in cognitive science called the correspondence concept; it means that what we teach should lead to kids having something in their head that corresponds more closely to what an expert has in her head. . . . Let's make sure we're teaching learners how experts actually read and write and make meaning. (Wilhelm and Butts 2018, 384–85)*

I find this description of experts so apt. Imagine dancers in the American Ballet Theatre—those expert artists could tell you *why* they did something in the midst of a dance and *how* they did it, and they can monitor and self-correct their practice. If an expert dancer loses her balance or doesn't rotate her spin as tightly as necessary, she knows precisely how to adjust or correct herself. Teachers are the reading experts in the room. We are the ones called upon to unpack the process of our craft. We must demonstrate for kids the strategies and mental models we use to read a book with deep comprehension so they can use corresponding strategies in their own reading.

Tip 4: Think Aloud

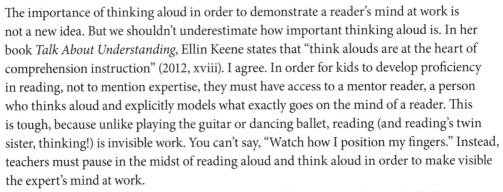

The importance of thinking aloud in order to demonstrate a reader's mind at work is not a new idea. But we shouldn't underestimate how important thinking aloud is. In her book *Talk About Understanding*, Ellin Keene states that "think alouds are at the heart of comprehension instruction" (2012, xviii). I agree. In order for kids to develop proficiency in reading, not to mention expertise, they must have access to a mentor reader, a person who thinks aloud and explicitly models what exactly goes on the mind of a reader. This is tough, because unlike playing the guitar or dancing ballet, reading (and reading's twin sister, thinking!) is invisible work. You can't say, "Watch how I position my fingers." Instead, teachers must pause in the midst of reading aloud and think aloud in order to make visible the expert's mind at work.

This pause is important (more on the power of the pause in Chapter 8, "Take a Breath"). In the same way that we take a moment to look up before starting the read-aloud every day, it is important to take a moment to differentiate between the reading aloud and the thinking aloud. Sometimes I watch teachers do beautiful think-alouds, but when I look around the classroom, it's clear some kids aren't sure whether the teacher is thinking aloud or still reading! This might seem like a minor point, but it's not. If we are going to pause to come out of the wonderful read-aloud experience, we must make it count, which means we must make sure all the kids are set up to adjust their thinking. We want make sure it's clear that we are now demonstrating our thinking minds at work or modeling a comprehension strategy. Whenever I pause to think aloud, I am careful to put the book down or set it aside. That simple action helps differentiate between "I'm reading" and "I'm showing you my thinking."

Equally important is making sure students know that while you are thinking aloud, they have plenty of active work to be doing: observing, listening, thinking, learning. Kids need plenty of opportunities to process, talk, and think together about the book, but when we do the think-aloud, for the most part, it means we are the only ones talking. I explain this to kids in a very straightforward way: "When I think aloud and show you my mind at work, I expect you to pay close attention to my reader's mind at work. I expect you to think alongside me, but for those moments, remember to keep your thinking alive in your minds, not aloud in the room! I promise I will give you lots of opportunities to talk. And you'll know it's your turn because I'll say, 'Turn and talk!'" Read-alouds can turn into a free-for-all if we are not clear about the boundaries. (And, not to confuse things, but there is a case for *some* read-alouds to actually be free-for-alls. Every now and then a read-aloud can be such raucous fun that it's impossible not to let things go a bit, especially if you are rereading well-loved or funny books with younger children.) The boundaries send a message that the thinking work you are demonstrating is important and kids should pay attention.

On the other side, it's important that we not talk too much. I am a talker, so this is something that I've struggled with. If we talk too much, we lose kids' attention and we take away from the read-aloud experience. Our teaching loses traction. The think-aloud becomes all about *us* and not at all about *them*! So I aim to make my think-alouds thoughtful and clear but *lean*, as Lucy Calkins taught me. I want to say something that matters, that gives the kids an explicit link to my reading mind at work. See Video 2 for an example.

This is obviously easier said than done. What exactly makes a worthy and valuable, not to mention lean, think-aloud? We can do a concise think-aloud for the students and still not do much for their reading lives. That is because "there is a real difference between superficial and deep understanding, and our talk in the classroom is the tool we use to bridge that gap" (Keene 2012, xix). Our think-alouds should be the expression of our reading expertise. But in order to make

Video 2
Read-Aloud
into
Think-Aloud

See p. ix on how to access this video clip and others found in the book.

and express meaning in sophisticated ways, we must be dedicated to the task of being real readers in the world. Dancers are not dancers because they *say* they are dancers. Dancers are dancers because they dance. The same is true for us. We cannot teach reading in powerful ways unless we are living rich reading lives.

Tip 5: Fuel Yourself

Anyone who has flown on an airplane knows you are supposed to put on your own oxygen mask before assisting someone else. Too often I think we teachers forget to put on our oxygen masks. We are a fiercely dedicated bunch and would do just about anything for our kids. But sometimes we forget to fill ourselves up. If one of the most important things we can give our students is a powerful model of an active, engaged reader, then one of our most important tasks is to stay active and engaged in our reading lives. I know you might think to yourself, "Wait, what? Take more time for myself to read? But I have so much to do for my students, my classroom, my lesson plans!" But I am saying to you, one of the most important things you can do for your students is to **read yourself**. My mom taught for thirty-eight years and I watched her spend weekends and summer vacations preparing, sorting, labeling, writing, responding, planning, and beautifying. Like all the best teachers I know, she was fiercely devoted to her students and had their needs, their projects, and their challenges on her mind constantly. But she also did something else that was equally important: she spent at least thirty minutes a day reading books of her own. My mom fueled herself and her teaching by putting her oxygen mask on.

All of us want our students to ask generative, thought-provoking questions, think deeply about the choices characters make, read with a critical stance, and more. And when we refine and deepen our own reading practice, talk to fellow readers, and keep our reading minds and muscles active and alive, we have so much more authentic knowledge and experience from which to teach. By pushing ourselves to read widely and deeply, ask questions, think carefully, and put together the threads of a book, we become better at reading. We begin to develop a stronger sense of what kind of thinking really pays off when we read, which we can then model with more acuity when we think aloud. Put simply, when we put our own oxygen masks on, we have so much more to offer our kids.

How to Fuel Yourself and Your Literary Life

Fuel your passion for literature, and find joy in reading. You will take that energy back with you and it will impact your kids.

- Gather with other teachers and start a book club! Read children's literature or contemporary authors and thinkers. Have snacks—obviously!

- Grow your knowledge of the books in your classroom library by setting goals or creating a stack of books you want to read over vacations and throughout the year.

- Listen to great books on Audible while you drive to work, do the dishes, wait in the grocery store line, and take a walk. (Some of my favorite listens have been *Eleanor Oliphant Is Completely Fine*, by Gail Honeyman, *Behold the Dreamers*, by Imbolo Mbue, and *Room*, by Emma Donoghue.)

- Check out podcasts and interviews with authors. I love learning about an author's process and inner life!

- Find a column or weekly blog post that you look forward to reading each week. (I love "By the Book," a weekly column in the *New York Times* where authors and other notable people discuss books and their lives as readers.)

- Text with your old high school pals about what you are reading as a way to catch up. My girlfriends and I from middle and high school are always doing this. It's one of the first things we talk about when we get together during our once-a-year reunions!

- Start a list of books that friends and colleagues have suggested so you always have an exciting queue to reference.

- Have a book-swap holiday party. I did this with my new friends in San Diego as a way to get to know them better and institute a little holiday cheer in my new (too-sunny) West Coast life. Now it's a new tradition!

(*continues*)

- Browse the shelves of fellow teachers' libraries and ask them about their favorite books. Take pictures on your phone to help you remember later.
- Browse the shelves of bookstores and read a few opening chapters. Again, take pictures on your phone to help you remember later.
- Follow authors you love on Instagram.

When I read, my teacher brain has a hard time shutting off. It has become habit now to read and think, "What am I noticing about the characters [or setting or language] so far? Why did the author make this choice or that?" By pausing to dig for meaning, I am laying the groundwork for future think-alouds. By deepening my own practice and observing my thoughts, even capturing them as I read with a quick jot, I am filling myself up with reading fuel. If our think-alouds are to have an impact on our children's learning and truly model what strong comprehension looks and sounds like, we need to work on the depth, substance, and clarity of our thinking so we can express it in ways that have traction and power.

At the end of the day, real reading is all about true understanding: what the words on the page mean and also what must be inferred. For more on the work of powerful think-alouds, read *Talk About Understanding* (Keene 2012) and make your own reading life a priority.

As you read children's literature in an effort to grow your knowledge of books inside your library, be aware of the shifting demands at different levels of texts and in different genres. The Teachers College Reading and Writing Project has taken a close look at how books fall into bands of text complexity, and this is extremely useful to consider when you are planning your read- and think-alouds. For one, it helps to know that we can think of books as part of a band of text complexity versus trying to wrap our heads around the minute differences between Lexile level 450 and Lexile level 675 or Guided Reading levels R and S. And secondly, it helps us know what we might shine a spotlight on as we read and think aloud. It's helpful to understand how to differentiate the thinking work we can do inside different bands of text complexity. And of course, we are often reading books aloud that are at much higher levels of text complexity than what children can read independently, allowing them to exercise thinking muscles they might not be applying in their independent reading lives. And we can model the thinking work that lots of kids *do* need practice with applying in their independent reading lives by reading aloud books that reflect different reading levels inside a classroom.

As I wrote this book, my twins were in first grade and they loved reading the hilarious, slapstick Mercy Watson books, by Kate DiCamillo. The Guided Reading level for Mercy Watson books is K, so they fall in the KLM band of text complexity. KLM books are often part of a series and they usually revolve around a fairly obvious problem and solution. Therefore, if I read aloud a KLM book, I will pause and think aloud about the character traits (how they act and feel, what they struggle with, what they love, and why they are making certain choices); what the problem seems to be in the story; my predictions for how the problem might be solved; and ideas about lessons the characters may have learned at the end. I'll model the way I pause at the end of each chapter to think about the big thing that happened so far in order to help kids remember that keeping track of a story over longer chapters and across more pages means pausing to hold onto the important information. I'll demonstrate how to track a story, retell the main events, think about how the problem was solved, and determine what the character(s) likely learned as a result.

For the most part, the work readers do when they independently read KLM books, or other series books like Mercy Watson, is practice accurate and fluent reading, tackle tricky words and phrases, learn new vocabulary, predict the way the problem might unfold and be solved, and retell the story afterward in order to hold onto important information and synthesize the key events.

But the work shifts as books move into higher Guided Reading levels. For example, books in band NOPQ require readers to think more inferentially, with careful attention to the world and characters that are being developed. You can no longer read with one problem in mind, pausing after every chapter to consider what might happen next to solve it. At the higher bands, there are often multiple, overlapping problems, and this is especially true as books get into the RST band and certainly in the UVW band and above, where the characters are even more multidimensional, the problems more intersectional, the solutions less clear-cut, and the interpretative work more open-ended.

For a more thorough exploration and the most up-to-date thinking about this topic, check out *Understanding Texts and Readers* (Serravallo 2018). In the meantime, read a range of children's literature, paying attention to the intellectual and emotional demands of the books as they get more difficult. There is no better way to get to know how the complexity shifts than by reading children's literature on your own or preferably with fellow colleagues!

Questions About Meaning Making to Keep in Mind as You Read Children's Literature

- What are you doing in order to create a strong mental picture and an understanding of who the characters are, where the book takes place, and what the big ideas or themes are?
- How do you have to pay attention differently in order to do to this as the books become more complicated?
- What questions do you have about what you are learning—either about a character, the time and place, the dynamics between characters, the surrounding context, or the way the problems are introduced?
- When do you pick up speed and when you do have to slow down?
- What do you notice about the work you must do to make sense of this world, these characters, these shifts in perspective or time?
- What work do you have to do to hold onto the important information or ideas?
- What do you notice about the way you read as the titles climb the ladder of complexity? What is confusing and what do you do about it?
- How does the reading experience feel different than it does when you read books at lower levels of text complexity?

Reading with a metacognitive stance simply helps us notice what we notice! We notice what helped us connect the dots; we notice when our picture got fuzzy and what we did about it; we notice how we constructed an opinion or a theory about something. The more we pay attention to our reading and nourish our reading lives, the better we become at *teaching* reading because we can dip into the informed well of ourselves. And our commitment to our students' reading lives also means getting to know the best of contemporary children's literature and staying current about books and authors that are out there.

Tip 6: Pay Attention to Significant Details *and* to Students' Responses

One of the reasons read-aloud is so crucial for upper-grade and middle school students is that it gives them access to books that are often very complicated, sometimes too complicated for them to read independently with true comprehension. Equally important, it gives them a road map for how to navigate through complex books. There is no doubt reading aloud is essential for all kids as they grow into harder books and learn strategies for comprehending and putting together the threads of more difficult texts. And, of course, for kids who struggle, read-aloud is a lifeline to ideas, themes, information, and conversations they are yearning to have but might not be able to access in the books they can independently read.

Think about what it's like to begin a new book. Sometimes you feel like you've been dropped in the middle of a world or place or perspective that feels altogether new, even confounding. It can be difficult to know where it's all heading, or why the author has laid it out the way she has. But experienced readers know what to look for, what clues or information to hold onto in order to make meaning and eventually put it all together. When we know what details to be alert for, we are able to make stronger connections, notice with greater insight, and ultimately make more meaning out of the experience. And, most importantly, we enjoy the experience more completely!

One of my favorite go-to analogies—and graphic organizers—that helps particularly with tackling increasingly complex books is something I call the Literary Backpack. I first learned of this strategy during my graduate school years, when I visited one of the most gifted teachers I've ever met, Kirsten Myers-Blake, in her fourth-grade classroom on the East Side of Manhattan. The Literary Backpack analogy helps me model the way readers slow down in the beginning of a new book to notice, take in, and collect in the backpack all of the new information coming at them. Readers very consciously fill up their backpacks with the small details that help them build the world of a story—a time and place, people, and a particular set of problems or conditions—which helps them make their way through a book with true understanding. It's essential to read with a wide-awake mind right from moment one. The Literary Backpack is a way to give readers practice at becoming active rather than passive consumers of text. Books (especially after levels KLM) are not going to do that work for us and sometimes we gotta work a little bit to get to the good stuff! The Literary Backpack helps me model *how* I might go about that. Here's how I usually introduce the idea:

> *I love to hike and whenever I go on a hike, I always prepare. I make sure my backpack is full of the things I need, like snacks, a sweatshirt, a compass, a trail map, water, and nowadays a charged phone, because I don't want to get a little ways down the path only to realize I have no idea where I'm going! I have no idea where I began! I'm having a terrible time because I'm cold, hungry, wet, and lost! Here's the thing: Hiking is a lot like reading. When we read, we want to feel like we are having a fabulous time as we journey through the woods of a book. In order for that to happen, it helps to pack what I like to call my Literary Backpack. Right from the very beginning of a book, I make sure I am paying careful attention to three things:*
>
> 1. *Who is in the story—what do I know and think about the characters?*
> 2. *What the problems seem to be—I'm usually on the lookout for more than just one and I'm thinking about how they might be connected.*
> 3. *What the setting is like—what details help me understand this time and place?*
>
> *In addition to those things, I'm also thinking about what issues this book seems to be tackling—what big ideas does this author seem to be addressing in this book? I don't want to wait to do that kind of thinking; I want to be alert right away to the possible themes and ideas that are living inside a book.*
>
> *And, finally, I pay attention to the questions I have. Because, as we know, when books get more complicated, they can sometimes be confusing. So it helps to*

name our confusion and jot our questions down in order to carry them with us as we read.

When we go a little slower in the beginning of a new, complicated book, we can fill our backpacks with important information that will help us make our way through a book. That way, we won't get to Chapter 4 or 5 and think, "I have no idea where I'm going! I'm having a terrible time because I'm cold, hungry, wet, and lost!" Instead, we'll think, "I'm having the best time on this journey through this book!"

Let's do this together as we read this new, more complicated book. As I read, I'll stop and think about what I'm adding to my backpack, and I'll ask you to think about what you might want to add as well.

When I first introduce the Literary Backpack tool with kids, I am more apt to model my thinking so they understand what my reader's mind is doing as I "pack my backpack" and begin my journey through a challenging book. Sometimes the only backpack chart is the one on the document camera or easel, and as kids turn and talk about what we should add I capture their thinking on the chart. Other times, I have the model up front and kids each have a journal or an organizer that they fill out with each other when they turn and talk. (See Figure 4.1 for a Literary Backpack organizer with my notes on how to fill in each section.)

I almost always keep a Literary Backpack visible throughout a read-aloud because it's a helpful reminder of the key information and, of course, most kids benefit from visual reminders of the story elements and big ideas. As the story or information evolves, the backpack serves as a touchstone and can be a perfect reminder of how our thinking has changed from the beginning of the book to the middle to the end. It's also a springboard for conversation: "Let's look back at our backpack. At the beginning of the book, we were wondering about [thinking about, noticing] . . . What new observations or ideas do we have about the characters [this place, these problems] now?"

Once kids are familiar with the backpack process, I often ask them to fill out a backpack organizer on their own—either at the start of a new read-aloud or for their independent, partnership, or club books—as a way to gather data about their thinking. What are they attending to as readers? What kinds of things are they noticing or wondering about?

Literary Backpack for TITLE OF BOOK_____ by AUTHOR NAME(S)_____

Characters

As I read, I model what I *know* about a character and what I *think* about a character. I capture information like "12 years old, oldest, loves school" and impressions like "She seems like a risk taker" or "Risk taker?" Because nothing is set in stone right away in complicated books, we have to keep adding, confirming, or revising as we go. There are often lots of characters in complicated books and listing them with quick jots is a super helpful tool for all kids but especially kids who need a visual support throughout the read-aloud.

(Possible) Problems

I make sure to write *possible* problems, because they may be ambiguous. We are on the lookout and things will reveal themselves as we continue through the book. But often authors plant seeds of problems right away and we can't miss those intentional seeds or we will end up confused later on.

Setting/Time and Place

As with characters, I keep track of explicit details like dates and names of places. But I also make sure to jot ideas about what the time or place *seems* to be like. I jot words that capture the mood or feeling of the place. I jot what I think, wonder, or notice.

Questions I'm Carrying

Right away, I model any questions I have to show how I deal with confusion in a complicated book. By jotting them down, I can carry them with me and stay on the lookout for information that will help me find answers or clarity. Our questions are an important measure of our thinking. We should be questioning and wondering as we go, right from the beginning!

(Possible!) Issues/Themes

Sometimes it's clear that a book will tackle big issues like friendship, discrimination, or grief, but it's helpful to show how we keep an eye out for the *potential* big themes right away so we can track them, watch how they evolve, and try to understand what the author might be trying to say about any one of them.

For a blank copy of the Literary Backpack, see the Online Resources (OR 4.1).

Figure 4.1 Annotated Literary Backpack

What kind of comprehension strategies might benefit them? (see Figures 4.2 and 4.3). Creating backpacks for new books in small groups is also a strategy you might use in order to support kids as they start more complicated books, even if you just talk about it together before they get too far along in the book. The point of this strategy, however, is not to teach children how to go off and make beautiful Literary Backpacks. It is a tool for helping them slow down and pay more careful attention to the details that are revealed from the start of a book so they can begin to build a new world inside their brains and read with deep comprehension. It is a tool to help them envision the text, look back across the book, revise their

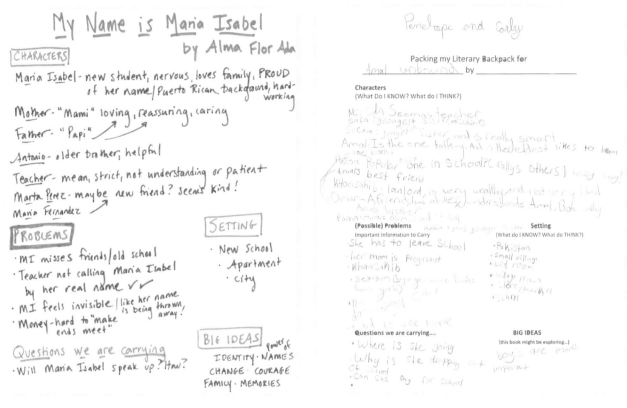

Figure 4.2 Literary Backpack from *My Name Is Maria Isabel* (Ada 1993)

Figure 4.3 Literary Backpack from *Amal Unbound* (Saeed 2018)

thinking, and actually enjoy the book. In short, it is a tool (like any other graphic organizer) in service of making meaning.

More than anything, making meaning is the whole point of reading. When we teach kids to read with wide-awake minds, we are really teaching them to move in the world with more awareness—to consider the details, to pay attention to an author's or a person's choices, to think about all the tiny, beautiful moments that make up a book, a piece of theatre or art, even a life. The stakes couldn't be higher, really. We are helping them to make meaning not only out of their books but also out of their own lives.

5

Principle Three

Stay Open
Making room for rich thinking

There's a deep and interesting kind of troubling that poems do, which is to say: "This what you think you're certain of, and I'm going to show you how that's not enough. There's something more that might be even more rewarding if you're willing to let go of what you already know." Literature allows us to be open, to listen, and to be curious.

—POET LAUREATE TRACY K. SMITH

Every day I'm in a classroom with children, watching them thinking and talking together, I almost always see or hear something that, in the words of Mary Oliver, "kills me with delight." This is what happens when we enter classrooms with an open stance and a willingness to let go of what we think we already know. When we read aloud, staying open to what the children are saying and thinking makes it possible to honor their unique perspectives on the stories we are sharing and the characters or information we are learning about in books. When we read to children, we lead them into new worlds. We want them to feel they are part of the meaning-making journey. Staying open to what they have to say sends a message that their voices and their ideas matter.

Staying open is essential to living in the world creatively. Artists come to the rehearsal room with a spirit of openness about the work they will do that day. Of course, they come prepared to do the work; they have read the script or practiced their musical part. But when they arrive at the rehearsal hall, they stay open to what their fellow actors are bringing to the scene or how a musical moment might be shaped by adjusting the tempo or volume.

Teachers do the same! We spend time reading the book, thinking about the story, reviewing a chapter. We mark places where we might ask a question or do some thinking aloud. We consider spots where our students might need a little extra support. This kind of prep work makes it possible to conduct the read-aloud with a spirit of openness. While reading, we are also looking and listening, ready to be delighted by what the children might say.

I have a lot of friends who are working actors. I have known Alison Cimmet since our college days, where we performed in shows like *Into the Woods* together. I've watched Alison go on to perform in multiple Broadway shows, and we have continued to collaborate on several artistic projects. I asked her about the connection between staying open during a read-aloud and staying open during a performance onstage. "Live theater is a shared experience," she wrote to me in an email, "and I need to be open in order for the show to be rich and alive and in-the-moment. There is a give and take between actors, musicians, audience, and even the technical elements of a show—that makes live theatre electric and exciting. Also, no matter how many times I've performed a show, I remind myself that it is this audience's first time seeing it. I owe it to them to stay present and open every single night" (June 20, 2017).

Alison's description of staying open every night even after performing a show again and again is similar to a teacher's quest to create a classroom that is also "electric and exciting"—with learning and conversation, new ideas and problem solving—even though we may have read a book many times. How do we keep our teaching, and our reading, alive? How do we help children feel they are on a path of discovery?

Tip 7: Pretend It's Your First Time Reading

The spirit of openness is at work from the moment I crack open a book in order to plan. Once I've chosen a book to read aloud (which is an important decision; see Chapter 12), I commit to reading and preparing that book before I begin the work in a classroom. I actually really love this moment when I take hold of a book that will be at the center of my classroom's world for a while. Because I've picked a book I love or feel will teach my kids important lessons, I am always eager to begin this process. So I try to read the book anew.

Even if you have read the book before, try to notice with new eyes and experience the text in a fresh way. It's always possible to add new layers of understanding or develop a more nuanced view of the story, the characters, the structure, or the author's choices. And growing ideas of your own, and creating an even stronger sense of the story and the characters, frees you to be more open to the children when it comes time to read to them. You can focus on the art of reading the book, listening to the children, and facilitating their thinking and experience.

Most importantly, though, it will help you remember to bring that same sensibility to the classroom when you begin the book. Starting a new book should feel like a special moment: there should be a bit of fanfare around the journey you are about to embark upon. After all, you will be gathering around this book as community for the next several weeks, developing thinking, listening, reading, and discussion skills along the way. So, when you take hold of that book, look for new ideas. Also try to recall what you love about the book, what makes it such a perfect choice to read to your class. Fill yourself up with renewed passion for the book so children can feed off of that! You want them to sit up straighter, lean in closer, and expect to be delighted.

When you read a book in your classroom, most likely you will have read this book before, perhaps many times. Try to remember, however, that this is the first time *these* children are hearing this story, or at least their first time hearing *you* read it. There is a singularity about this reading, with this class, on this day. And, just as Alison described earlier, we owe it to the students to stay present and open every single time we read aloud. If we do, we will also find ourselves responding in authentic ways. John Douglas Thompson, one of the greatest classical actors working in American theatre right now, echoes this idea perfectly. While Thompson was performing the epic role of Othello in New York City, he talked about how he "live[d] within the play and [wasn't] certain that he [would] kill Desdemona until the moment he [did]" (Wilkinson 2012). That almost sounds impossible, right? Of course Thompson knew how the play was going to end and what his character would say and do, but he stayed fully present inside each moment as he lived them. "I know what's coming," he said, "but I don't know how it's going to fashion itself. Instead, I'm conscious of where I am—what my scene partner is doing, or what I'm hearing, and I know that I need to respond. I believe I have a chance to change the outcome. My wife is going to reveal the truth to me, or I'm going to wake up and realize it's not possible that she can be unfaithful" (Wilkinson 2012).

It might seem odd to compare performing one of the most demanding, complicated stage roles ever written to reading a children's book, but I find great resonance between it and living inside a story that I'm reading aloud. Because even though I know exactly what Opal is going to say after she hears ten things about her mama, for instance, I try to "stay conscious" and stay open to whatever she is going to reveal.

In *Because of Winn-Dixie*, when Opal finally says, "I wanted to know those ten things inside and out. That way, if my mama ever came back, I could recognize her, and I would be able to grab her and hold on to her tight and not let her get away from me again" (DiCamillo 2000, 30), I am always struck by the heartbreaking significance of that sentiment. I try to read those lines so that kids can observe a real reader in real time, experiencing the weight of those words. By stepping inside that moment along with Opal and listening to those ten things about Mama along with her, I can't help but feel swept away by the beauty and sorrow of her final words. Every time I read those words, I experience the full weight of Opal's longing and loss, and every time, something happens in the room, something intangible but profound. By staying open, we stay fresh. We make it possible for students to truly understand the tremendous power words can have in our lives.

Tip 8: Stay Curious the Whole Time

Staying open also means to *expect* to be blown away by children's insights, their quirky ways of saying things, and their wisdom. You will inevitably discover new ideas, new ways of thinking about a particular part, or character, or author's purpose. Children are nothing if not completely unique in the way they respond to or think about things. Their unfiltered imaginations and capacity for thinking in original ways never fail to surprise me. And it is wonderful to be surprised, to be intrigued by what a child says, to see or hear something that more or less kills you with delight! That is what keeps our teaching rich and alive.

When I work in schools or lead workshops, sometimes I end up reading the same book back-to-back, which could be tedious. In reality, I always find it interesting because I am eager to hear the responses of the children or participants. I don't have a specific expectation for what they are going to say. I read with an air of expectancy, of course, but with an open stance that leaves room for multiple possibilities. Essentially, *I stay curious the whole time.* I allow my curiosity to lead me through the read-aloud, and children sense that I am really listening to them and taking in what they have to say.

One of my favorite picture books to read aloud to both upper-grade students and teachers is *Fox* (Wild 2006). *Fox* is stunning to read and look at and endlessly fascinating to discuss because there are so many potential interpretations and ideas to consider. The conversation one day is often completely different than that on another. For one cycle of read-alouds, I asked these questions after the reading every time: "What are some of the big ideas you see inside *Fox*? What do you think Margaret Wild might have been trying to say about one (or more) of these ideas?" Students discussed the big ideas and chose one to explore before developing a theme statement. As a class, we brainstormed ideas that Wild seemed to be exploring and charted them. (See Figure 5.1.)

In partnerships and small groups, students then developed interpretative statements about what Wild might have been trying to say about any of those ideas. As a class, we shared out those statements and created a new chart. After every workshop, the chart looked completely different. All three classes had different outcomes, all of which could be supported and were rich with meaning (see Figures 5.2, 5.3, and 5.4). Most importantly, it didn't matter to me what ideas or theme statements students created; it mattered that they were doing rich interpretative work and pushing themselves to think deeply. It mattered to me that students were supporting their ideas through conversation about the book.

I delight in the language and original ways students wrap thinking around an idea inside a book. This is not to be underestimated. When you model your delight, kids learn an essential lesson: that they are members of the great literacy club (Smith 1987) and that reading is both an expansive and a joyful experience. Discovering the joy of reading and thinking fuels children's desire to read independently, and it encourages them to bring the same spirit of thinking, wondering, imagining, and questioning to their own books.

Figure 5.1 Big Ideas Inside *Fox*

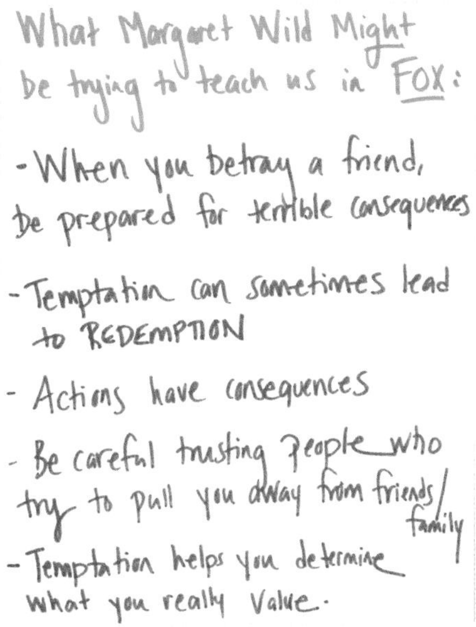

What Margaret Wild Might
be trying to teach us in FOX:

- When you betray a friend,
be prepared for terrible consequences

- Temptation can sometimes lead
to REDEMPTION

- Actions have consequences

- Be careful trusting people who
try to pull you away from friends/
family

- Temptation helps you determine
what you really value.

Figure 5.2 Chart from Classroom 1 (Notice how this classroom was caught up in the idea of temptation and betrayal, which other classrooms didn't attend to nearly as much!)

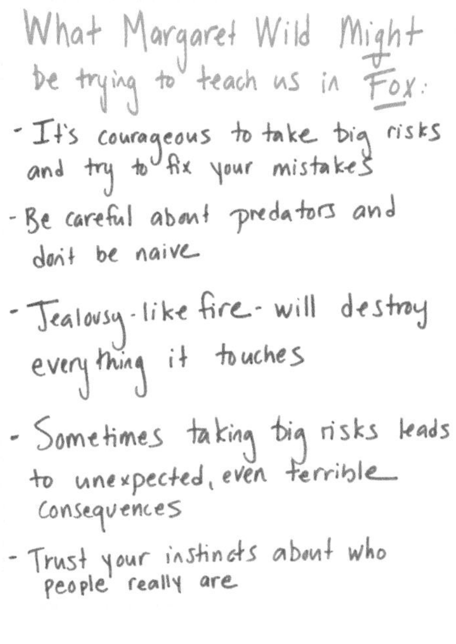

What Margaret Wild Might
be trying to teach us in Fox:

- It's courageous to take big risks
and try to fix your mistakes

- Be careful about predators and
don't be naive

- Jealousy· like fire· will destroy
everything it touches

- Sometimes taking big risks leads
to unexpected, even terrible
consequences

- Trust your instincts about who
people really are

Figure 5.3
Chart from
Classroom 2

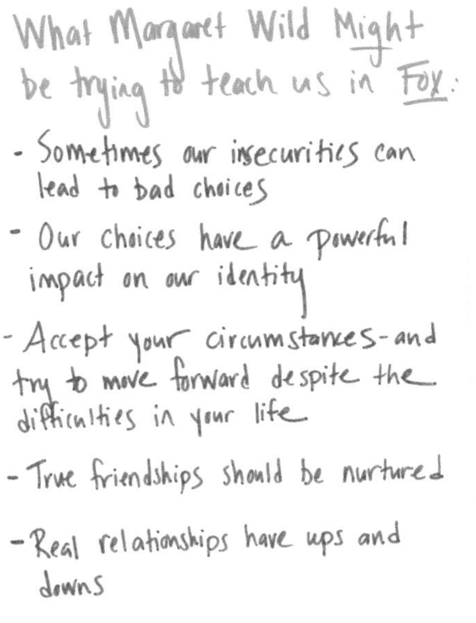

What Margaret Wild Might
be trying to teach us in Fox:

- Sometimes our insecurities can
lead to bad choices

- Our choices have a powerful
impact on our identity

- Accept your circumstances- and
try to move forward despite the
difficulties in your life

- True friendships should be nurtured

- Real relationships have ups and
downs

Figure 5.4
Chart from
Classroom 3

Tip 9: Resist the Urge to Confirm Correctness

As I read books with children, I have my own ideas about the characters, the themes, and the author's message. There is also key information I want students to understand. But I try hard not to cling to my interpretations when I invite children to talk about the book because kids know the difference between questions that have right answers and questions that leave room for multiple points of view. Paula Denton (2007) writes that questions that are "open-ended" power academic and social learning:

> When we fish for specific answers, children soon realize we're not really asking for their thoughts, knowledge, or perceptions, but for them to articulate our own. Many then stop thinking and become less engaged. Or they respond by guessing wildly at the answer the teacher wants.

Staying open means we do more than just ask kids to confirm what *we* think about a book. It means we give students a chance to find that needle of light inside the haystack of a book. We let them try out new words and think creatively. We also honor the attempts students are making to construct meaning by acknowledging their viewpoints, letting them talk with partners, and allowing them time to process or think.

The truth is, thinking takes time (more on this in Chapter 8). The read-aloud should be a protected time of day where kids feel encouraged to try things out, take risks, and wonder aloud, without worrying about getting it "right." Instead of evaluating a child's idea by saying, "Good," or "Exactly," you can simply repeat or rephrase what she said.

A few years ago, I read the wonderful book *My Name Is Maria Isabel* (Ada 1993) to a third-grade class at Marshall Elementary in San Diego's City Heights neighborhood. As I usually do, I stopped after Chapter 2 and asked them what they were noticing about what was happening for Maria Isabel. After I allowed students to turn and talk for a minute or two, I gathered them back together to share some of the ideas I had overheard.

Rebecca: I'm hearing a lot of you talk about how Maria Isabel is being treated at this new school, and this group was saying, "They're not really showing that they care about her. . . . They didn't introduce her to the class. They didn't ask what happened to her knee or dress. And, they aren't calling her by her real name."

I left a little space for thinking after naming out these important ideas. I could see the kids mulling this over when Raphael raised his hand.

Raphael: It's kind of like she's invisible.

Rebecca: It's like she's invisible. . . . Can you say more about that?

Raphael: Well, no one is asking what happened to her, or introducing her to the class.

Rebecca: Hmm. Let's all think in our brains about this powerful word Raphael just used. "It's like she's invisible." Why do you think he might be saying that? Why might that be true? Turn and talk!

This was an aha moment for me. The word *invisible* hadn't occurred to me, but it certainly made sense and led the class into a focused and passionate conversation about what was going on for Maria Isabel. By making space to discuss Raphael's idea, I showed the kids that the ideas inside a story don't belong to me, but to all of us. This notion that Maria Isabel was *invisible* resonated deeply with the kids, was rooted in the text, and would ultimately thread its way throughout our conversations about the book.

There are a few important considerations to keep in mind about this classroom moment. The first is how I set up the conversation. I asked a question that made room for many possible observations. Simple and open-ended questions (What do you think about what's happening here for Maria Isabel?) are enough to get kids thinking, wondering, and talking. Listening in to the kids' conversations helps me develop a stronger sense of who each child is. And it also gives me so much important information! What are the children attending to, thinking about, holding onto? What do I notice about the way different children respond and what does that tell me about who they are as readers, thinkers, talkers? How does all that (on-the-go) data inform my future instruction, both for the class and for individual students?

One of the most important takeaways from this classroom moment, however, is that I lifted up Raphael's actual words for the class to consider. I treated them as prized ideas. Instead of saying, "Yes, that's right," or "Good idea!" I mirrored his idea using a tone of voice that demonstrated I was eager to hear more and truly understand. Repeating back what a child has said gives everyone time to think, refine, and support the idea, or perhaps even discard it altogether. Mirroring a child's words is a way of honoring a child's thinking; it's a way of letting them know you hear them, you see them, you value them.

But what if the words kids say don't seem as dazzling or as rich with meaning as *invisible*? We must meet kids where they are. We can lift up children's words and invite them to wrap more thinking around their attempts at analysis. Think of a child learning to play the violin and imagine the first sounds she would make. When children are beginning the work of critical and deep thinking, it may not sound so dazzling at first. But we must invite children to spend a moment finessing the idea. After time, they can reach for more sophisticated words, ideas, and interpretations. But in the meantime, listen, look, and stay open to what your children bring to the table.

In addition to mirroring kids' words, I also try to help children elaborate their thinking by sticking with them and staying open to what they are trying to bring forth. Instead of evaluating children's answers, I often follow up with a question that helps them strengthen their initial ideas:

Why do you think that?

Can you say more about that?

What do we think about that idea?

Why do you think Raphael is using that word here?

Does someone else think the same?

Does someone else think something different?

In Video 3 I use a version of those questions with fourth graders at Adams Elementary School and middle schoolers at Grant Middle School.

Teachers often ask me what to do when, as occasionally happens, children offer up ideas that are off, misguided, or frankly just plain wrong. "How do we stay open to a child's idea when that idea makes no sense?" they ask. "Isn't it important that their thinking is supported in the text?" I believe that we must help children develop a keen sense for what the best answer or interpretation most likely is. We must help them read analytically and closely so that they can ground their theories with details and quotes from the books. And there are absolutely moments during our read-aloud conversations when I ask kids to think more about a claim they have offered or ask them what in the book gave them their idea.

But if we focus *only* on "correctness" and supporting our ideas with evidence from the text, we might not be nurturing a child's desire to read. The read-aloud should be a time where we protect the sanctity of listening, thinking, and wondering without the pressure of necessarily having the "right answer." While other times of a balanced literacy day should be a time for *evaluation*, the read-aloud should focus more on *invitation*. It should be a time

Video 3
Questioning with an Open Stance

See p. ix on how to access this video clip and others found in the book.

where children experience the joy of reading, of story, and of thinking and talking to one another because, simply put, all of that fuels their engagement in reading.

By staying open during our read-alouds, we are staying open to the very children in front of us. We are sharpening our sense for who these children are as readers, thinkers, and growing people. It makes our reading, and our reading *aloud,* better, but it also makes our listening and teaching better. It gives us more insight into the text and also our students. It allows us to let go of what we think we are certain about and understand something, or someone, anew.

6

Principle Four

Look Up

Connecting and making eye (and heart!) contact

The process of getting in a room with people and making
something is so immediate, as is the rush of when you perform
it live. . . . There's nothing like it, the honesty of that exchange.
When you're a performer, all you want to do is connect.

—LIN-MANUEL MIRANDA

In my work with teachers, I hear over and over again that they went into teaching because they love kids and that the best part about their job is the feeling of connection with their students. Connection is at the root of the entire enterprise of teaching. The relationships between teachers and kids are central to academic success and positive outcomes across the board. This is supported by boatloads of evidence. In their book *Creative Schools*, Robinson and Aronica write, "The heart of education is the relationship between the student and the teachers. Everything else depends on how productive and successful that relationship is" (2015, 71). Zaretta Hammond writes extensively about the "real science" behind the link between relationships and learning:

> *When we feel cared for, our brain is flooded with neurotransmitters and hormones like oxytocin, the same hormone that makes moms fall in love with their babies even after the pain and effort of labor. These "happy chemicals" tell our prefrontal cortex, the thinking part of the brain, that all is safe socially, emotionally and*

physically. All systems are a go for learning. What happens if you don't feel safe or cared for? Ain't no learning happening. Imagine going through school without feeling affirmed for the way you speak, think or see the world? I can bet that doesn't generate a lot of happy feelings. Instead, you might feel guarded, untrusting and a wee bit hostile even. (2013a)

There is so much going on in our schools that distracts from the needs of children and the essential work of teaching and learning—our focus on standards and test scores chief among them. It is easy to forget that at the end of the day, nothing is more important to young people than the relationships they have with their teachers. Those connections create the conditions for children to do their best learning and become their best, most engaged, inquiring, motivated, imaginative, and wholehearted selves. It creates the space for meaningful, genuine connection and its effects ripple out throughout the rest of the day. It solidifies the bonds you have with one another as both a learning and a reading community, and it creates a culture around books like nothing else.

With our pervasive screen culture, looking down has become the new normal these days, but *looking up* is the work of artists and teachers. In order to teach well, we have to see who is in front of us. In order to truly understand who a child is, what motivates him and makes him tick, what lights her up or helps unlock a particular challenge, we have to observe and listen. There is no app to do that work for us. There is no app for creating the kind of honest exchange Lin Manuel describes in the opening quote either. When you are creating a piece of theatre, it's all about connecting—with one another, the text and story, the audience. Watch any orchestra, choir, dance company, or musical ensemble in the midst of a rehearsal or performance. The members of any artistic group must look closely at each other in order to perform the piece of work effectively, beautifully, and with intention.

Now, let's be honest, reading aloud to children is not the same as seeing or performing *Hamilton* live, but the same rush Miranda describes happening when you get into a room together to perform something is possible when you read aloud to a group of kids. In effect, your students can become your scene partners, your fellow collaborators and creators. In those minutes, you are doing the real and immeasurable work of artists: you are seeking to understand, to find meaning, to grow, and to feel inspired. As you read, you are relishing those opportunities to reach across the space between you and your kids and connect,

to look out and look up into the faces of the children in front of you. This part of the day is about seeing and being seen—for all of you.

Tip 10: Make Students Your Scene Partners

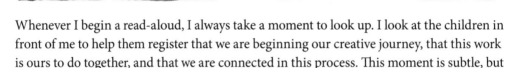

Whenever I begin a read-aloud, I always take a moment to look up. I look at the children in front of me to help them register that we are beginning our creative journey, that this work is ours to do together, and that we are connected in this process. This moment is subtle, but it creates a mood and informally ritualizes the experience.

It's tempting to just get started, to ask a question, to jump into the book, to move things forward. But taking a moment to look up signals to them that we are shifting into that time of day where we imagine, listen, and think together. Scanning the room also reminds us to take the kids in and connect. Kids are almost always quite eager to begin listening to a read-aloud so it's a perfect opportunity to share a moment of quiet anticipation together.

Scanning the room in this way reminds me of how it feels when the lights go down in the theatre or the conductor takes his place on the podium, baton held aloft. "Something magical is about to take place," we all feel in the audience. When we look out at the kids in this anticipatory way, we don't have to say anything with words. We are setting an intention. *Something beautiful is about to happen here.*

As you read fiction, there are innumerable moments when characters speak to one another, and often those moments, ripe with significance, present the perfect opportunity to pull your kids in even closer. With a simple shift, you can turn those moments into something more than a read-aloud—something more like real theatre—because you can invite your seven-year-olds or even thirteen-year-olds to be your scene partners. You can do this for any scene, at any time in a book.

Even moments that aren't significant, like when the manager of the Winn-Dixie grocery store gives Opal a "hard stare like maybe [she] was making fun of him" (DiCamillo 2000, 10), are great opportunities to pull your kids closer. Give a few of the kids a hard stare. Then, when the manager says, "Don't you know not to bring a dog into a grocery store?"

(DiCamillo 2000, 11), be the manager once again and look at another child or two as you ask that, rendering them Opal as well. While the scene between Opal and the manager is a fun, sort of silly moment, it helps lay the foundation for scenes that come later in the book that ask a bit more of you, like when Opal finally confronts her father about losing her mom, or when Sarah apologizes to Jerome in *Ghost Boys* for her father's actions or when Ghost's coach confronts him about the sneakers in Jason Reynold's *Ghost.* By making kids your scene partners, you heighten the drama, but you also give kids access to the nuances inside the scene, helping them make inferences and dive a little deeper into the motivations and experiences of the characters. Students feel a part of the book and build a stronger sense for what is transpiring between characters, even for the unspoken details inside a scene.

Whenever I read aloud, I am always shifting my focus, looking out into the group of kids and making eye contact, talking to them as though they are on the other side of the conversation in the text. Some teachers find this strategy a bit challenging at first because there is more looking up from the book than they are used to. It takes a bit of practice to constantly shift your focus away from the insides of the book to the kids in front of you. Even though it's possible to do a perfectly fine read-aloud without looking up in this way, creating real moments while you read aloud turns a read-aloud that is fine into one that is *artful*—truly engaging and compelling.

As you watch the scene in Video 4, notice the way I switch between Betty and Annabelle, making my students my scene partners as I read the scene from *Wolf Hollow* (Wolk 2016) where they first encounter one another in the woods.

Video 4
Make Students Your Scene Partners

See p. ix on how to access this video clip and others found in the book.

Tip 11: Show Them They Matter

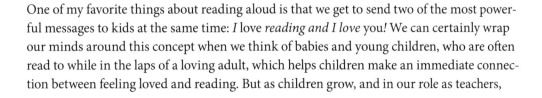

One of my favorite things about reading aloud is that we get to send two of the most powerful messages to kids at the same time: *I love reading and I love you!* We can certainly wrap our minds around this concept when we think of babies and young children, who are often read to while in the laps of a loving adult, which helps children make an immediate connection between feeling loved and reading. But as children grow, and in our role as teachers, how can we continue to make a link between loving reading and loving them? Kids can be seriously exhausting and sometimes it's all too easy to forget how truly lovely and little they are, even the fourteen-year-olds, who often tower over me. But give me a great book and a deep breath, and we can find our way back to each other and all can be well in the world.

During a read-aloud, students' faces almost always have a look of wonder and rapt attention—even the ones who just fifteen minutes before were pushing boundaries. Reading aloud always makes it possible for me to love my kids back up, even the ones who are in pesky moods or full of trouble on any given day. Sometimes I think the interactive read-aloud is even more important for those kids, because their moods and trouble making are often the manifestation of deep trouble in their lives, and more than anything they need to feel connected, seen, and loved through an experience that is engaging and freeing. Reading aloud helps all of us see kids once again for what they are: young people trying to figure a lot of things out and yearning to feel understood and loved.

There are numerous ways teachers can show students they matter. Reading aloud is one way, but it is important to remember that it depends on the authenticity of the connections, not how polished your performance is. While you are reading, take a moment to find the eyes of your kids and have a laugh, shake your head in disbelief, or sigh with relief. Let the kids know they are a meaningful part of this experience. These little moments of connection really add up.

Looking up also pulls students even closer into the action and world of the book. They feel drawn in, and the transaction between your book reading and their mind work deepens. Those little moments of connection are silent signals that reinforce literary thinking, informally holding them accountable for doing the work along with you. When you look up at them, you are silently communicating the following:

"I can't believe he is finally going to give this a shot. Can you?"

"I wonder what will happen next. Do you?"

"I'm feeling something so big here. What are you feeling?"

"Wow, that felt significant! Did you notice that too?"

One of my all-time favorite stories about the power of an adult reading aloud to a child is documented in *The Reading Promise*, by Alice Ozma (2012). Alice's dad, Jim, had stopped reading aloud to her older sister, Kathy, when she was in fourth grade, but he didn't

want that time to end with his younger daughter. As a result, when Alice was in fourth grade, Jim suggested a challenge: he would read aloud to her for one hundred nights in a row. After celebrating one hundred days, Alice and Jim upped the ante and began what they called "the Streak," which they decided would last a thousand days. This suggestion came during a time of painful family upheaval as well. "It was just the two of us," Alice remembers. "The Streak was stability when everything else was unstable. It was something I knew would always be there. People kept leaving me, but with The Streak, I knew that nothing would come before The Streak. In high school, I had friends who never talked to their parents. It never occurred to me not to. If someone takes care of you, you want to be with them" (Winerip 2010).

Jim ultimately read aloud to Alice for 3,218 days, culminating with the book that they'd read together first, *The Wizard of Oz*, on Alice's first day of college. The details are in the book, including the rules for the Streak (e.g., he had to read at least ten minutes a day), but at the root of this story is the way in which reading aloud became a source of comfort, connection, and ultimately love.

While we might not be able to read to our students for 3,218 days straight, we can read to them for well over 100! Reading every day shows kids that they deserve to be part of something enjoyable and meaningful. It is a gift to us too, frankly, to have those bonds with our students strengthened. It feels good to know that for at least those several minutes a day, I will fall back in love with each and every one of them! How could I not when there they are, with their heads cocked, their eyes alight, their mouths open? How could I not when I share a sly grin with one of them or a look of shock with another?

Tip 12: Allow Yourself to Be Seen

If people argue that there isn't time in the day for all this kumbaya business, I inform them of all the research laid out in the opening chapter and in other chapters in this book as to why reading aloud is deeply instructional in and of itself. While it is instructional, it is also a time where we should lead with our hearts! We can model for kids how important it is to feel, to empathize, to be both brokenhearted and wholehearted all at once. We can be willing to be seen; kids can watch *us* being emotionally courageous and openhearted.

Kate DiCamillo describes the experience of her mother reading aloud Beverly Cleary's book *Ribsy* when she was nine:

> We sat on the Florida room couch. My mother was in the middle. My brother sat on one side of her and I sat on the other. Our dog, Nanette, slept at our feet as our mother read aloud. . . . I was transported by the story, but even more, I was moved by seeing my mother so undone, so human, so herself. I laughed at her laughing, and she looked down at me and laughed at my laughing. And my brother laughed at both of us laughing, and Nanette raised her head off the floor to stare at all of us laughing together. It was a wondrous thing. It was almost like we were getting to know one another, better, more deeply, through the story. (2015)

I love everything about DiCamillo's love letter to reading aloud here, especially what she says about being so moved by seeing her mother "so undone, so human, so herself." Kids need to see the grown-ups in their lives being themselves, being fully human, and even being a little undone sometimes. We need to let them in on the full range of human feelings that a story inspires in us, even if that means reading through the sadness, the yearning, and the heartbreak.

If you've ever read the ending of *Charlotte's Web* (White 2012), you'll know that it's virtually impossible to get through Charlotte's final hours without full-on weeping. I know it's coming and it still brings me to my knees. If I read that aloud to anyone, I am going to cry. But here's the thing: Great books are usually not stories of someone wanting something and then getting it, with no wrinkles and no problems. They are about big struggles and loss, grief, and a yearning to belong or feel understood. They are about being vulnerable and afraid but finding a way through it anyway.

When we read great books to kids, our hearts are going to be on the line. We are going to laugh and gasp; we will show our worry and concern. But it's not such a bad thing to be vulnerable. Brene Brown, who has a PhD in social work, writes and speaks extensively about courage, connection, and the importance of vulnerability. "Vulnerability is not weakness," Brown (2012) says in a TED talk.

> *That myth is profoundly dangerous. . . . I define vulnerability as emotional risk [and] uncertainty. It fuels our daily lives. . . . Vulnerability is our most accurate measurement of courage . . . to let ourselves be seen. . . . Vulnerability is the birthplace of innovation, creativity and change.*

If we are asking children to grow up to be leaders, thinkers, and agents of change and innovation, we need to teach them to do more than get answers right on tests. We need to teach them how to connect with others, be compassionate, engage with feelings, take risks, and think creatively. This is big work. We must lead the way and model what emotional courage looks like. We have the opportunity to help children understand that embracing big feelings and showing vulnerability are not weaknesses but signs of a healthy, wholehearted adult.

I'm not advocating that we need to full-on weep as we read books to kids, but we should allow ourselves to be seen by our kids as we read aloud. Artists are artists because they are willing to put themselves on the line, to create something that the world has most likely not asked them to create. Talk about vulnerability. Teachers can do the same. Helping kids become human beings who are able to connect and become wholehearted is actually one of the most important gifts we can give them. But we must be willing to be seen ourselves, and the read-aloud can help us do that.

7

Principle Five

Invite Conversation
Helping kids learn to talk and listen well

**Listening as an act of love is so much more than
being quiet while the other person speaks.**

—KRISTA TIPPETT

The summer I first moved to New York City, my mother and her teaching colleagues enrolled in the Lincoln Center Institute's course on arts in education. I would meet my mom and her friends on their lunch breaks and they would talk about the beautiful music the string musicians played for them or describe the dance moves they had learned that morning and then crack up over their salads and iced teas about how ridiculous they must have looked moving across the room as the drums beat. It sounded like heaven to me. I always dreamed of attending myself, and fifteen years later, I finally did. I'll never forget the way in which the instructors invited us into thoughtful conversation about the art we saw and experienced—especially experiences that were outside our comfort zones.

Unlike my mom and her friends, I had no trouble dancing along to the drums or performing in a small group. But the day came when we all headed to the Metropolitan Museum of Art to do a visual art workshop, and there I was, decidedly outside my comfort zone. I am not one of those people who looks at a painting or sculpture and feels I have anything smart to say.

On the day of our museum field trip, we met at Jackson Pollock's *Autumn Rhythm Number 30* and right away, I thought, "Uh-oh." *Autumn Rhythm Number 30* is an enormous painting on its own wall. I grew anxious as we gathered near it. Whatever we were supposed to be thinking, I was pretty sure I wouldn't be thinking it. But then the instructor did an amazing thing: he asked us to look at the painting and *think about what we noticed*. That's it. "What do you notice about the colors?" he continued. "What about the shapes on the canvas? Take a minute to think about your noticings and then describe what you see with a colleague."

Well, this was something I could do. And there was a lot for me to notice. Suddenly, I wasn't worried about being right; I was focused on trying to see. I felt free to think, excited to share what I saw and to hear what my partner had noticed that I had not. Once we were given the signal to talk, the room was abuzz. When we brought our attention back to the painting and the instructor, we spent some time building upon the noticings, which ultimately led to a conversation about Pollock's process, the significance of the piece, and the ideas Pollock was trying to convey. By the end of the conversation, I felt like I really knew that painting and that I had begun to understand a bit about how it was made and why.

Looking back at this experience, I am struck by how differently it all could have gone. Imagine if he had asked, "What is this painting trying to convey or teach us?" or "What are the most important elements of this painting?" I would have been frozen with anxiety and uncertainty. Those questions have right answers, or at least they appear to. I would have been so worried about looking foolish that my responses would have been a stab in the dark or an attempt to cover up what I didn't know. I would have felt defensive, not open. Guarded, not curious.

But the words "What do you notice?" open a world of possibility. They are a welcoming invitation to conversation. And they create a foundation for even deeper comprehension, analysis, interpretation, and evaluation.

When we read aloud, we look closely at a text—sometimes a text as confusing or sophisticated as a painting like *Autumn Rhythm*. The conversations we invite children to have with one another have a profound impact on their comprehension, engagement, and even independent reading lives. Our job is to welcome children to the thinking table in ways that make them eager to dig for true understanding, grow knowledge, and listen carefully through talk that is meaningful, purposeful, and powerful.

Tip 13: Create Opportunities for Talk

Conversation is a key piece of the interactive read-aloud. In her book *Teaching Talk*, Kara Pranikoff lays out why teaching talk is so important and describes the research that emphasizes the vital role talk plays in classrooms and learning. She shares a study by Douglas Fisher and Nancy Frey that found "the amount of talk that students do is correlated with their achievement" and ultimately that "talking something through facilitates understanding" (2017, xxvi).

It stands to reason that talking through something facilitates understanding. I think most people would agree that the most common way we work through problems, reach for solutions, and grow new thinking is through conversation. As Pranikoff writes, "conversation is the currency of most ideas in the world" (2017, xxix). And all of us who work with children know that most of them like to talk. Some more than others, and some with astonishing persistence. My twins are six, and my head is often spinning with how much they talk. It's like talking is their *job*. As I drive and they philosophize in the backseat, I secretly think, "Go to it kids! Talk it out! Figure out this perplexing and amazing world by examining it at full volume, asking every question, hashing it all out!"

The read-aloud is one of the best, most obvious times in our day to create space for rich and meaningful conversations. Kids are gathered and focused together on a text to which everyone has access. And if it's a well-chosen text, one that deeply engages their interest, kids will be eager to talk about what they are noticing, thinking, wondering, and predicting.

The questions I ask to spark read-aloud conversation don't change much over time. This is a relief: we don't have to puzzle over determining the best questions for each particular text. Pranikoff writes, "The strength of well written text, fiction or nonfiction, is that it propels student reflection and thinking on its own. Teachers do not need to labor over the perfect question to stimulate thinking. The text itself is stimulus for the creation of ideas. We just need to pause, with purpose, and give students the floor" (2017, 32). The questions I ask over and over again are often some iteration of the following five.

What are you noticing?

What new information are you learning?

What are you thinking?

What are you wondering?

What new ideas are you starting to grow?

Figure 7.1 shows how these questions might evolve across bands of text complexity, and from the text's beginning to end. Much of this thinking comes from the years I spent learning and teaching along with Lucy Calkins, Mary Ehrenworth, and other colleagues at the Teachers College Reading and Writing Project.

Creating opportunities for children to talk is different from creating opportunities for children to be called upon or heard. Children need to talk because "talking something through facilitates understanding" (Fisher and Frey 2014, 19). When children turn and talk to a partner, they must sift through their observations and ideas, which helps them make sense of the text. Every single child needs and deserves an opportunity to talk, but not every single child needs (or wants) to be heard by the whole class. It is crucial to teach that the value is in the talk itself, not in validation for being singled out or correct. We all know this is hard. When I have a great idea, I want to hear those exquisite words, "You're right! You're so smart!" But we must get children used to the idea that they are talking not to please us, but because it helps them become more thoughtful and astute readers. The talking kids do with each other extends beyond the read-aloud time and begins to have a profound effect on the conversations they have with *themselves* as they read. That is the lifelong conversation that all of us strive to deepen and make more meaningful—the one we have in our own brains as we read, discover, and learn.

A word of caution, though: If we allow the talking to go on too long, we will never get through any books. Most of the time, I make sure my turn-and-talks are brief. We read, we notice, we think, and we come up for air and have a quick turn-and-talk to clarify and solidify. Sometimes I think of the initial turn-and-talks as microconversations.

Figure 7.1 Turn-and-Talk Questions as You Move Up the Ladder of Complexity

Band of Text Complexity	Questions
K L M	
Beginning	• What are you noticing about the characters? How might you describe them? • What do you think the big problem is going to be in this book?
Middle/ As You Read	*At level KLM, characters stay pretty consistent throughout the story, so I focus more on how the problem is changing and how the characters are feeling as way of keeping track of the story as it develops, which is the big work through level M.* • What are you noticing about how this problem is changing? What do you think is going to happen? How are the characters going to solve their problem? • What are the big things that happened in this chapter/in this part that we should make sure to hold onto?
End	• What do you think about how the characters solved their problem? What do you think they learned? • Let's retell what happened in the story across our fingers from beginning to end! Turn and tell a partner. You can use *first, then, next, then,* and *finally.* *Or I might give them this frame:* 1. A character wanted . . . 2. But . . . 3. Then . . . 4. So . . . !

Figure 7.1 *Continued*

NOPQ

Beginning	*As we get into N and above, characters and stories/problems become more complicated, so after establishing some baseline ideas, I want to push for more; I want kids to practice pushing past their initial ideas and considering more than one idea at a time. Also, there is usually a lot more to notice and think about than a few descriptive character traits or a central problem, which would suffice in KLM. This is true for all the books above N. Helping kids to consider multiple possibilities is important, so make sure to read on and ask again, "What else are you learning/noticing/paying attention to that seems important?"* • What are you noticing about these characters? *What else are you noticing or wondering?* • What do you think some of the problems might be in this book? *What else?*
Middle/ As You Read	• What are you thinking or wondering about these characters and this relationship *now*? • What new ideas are you developing about the characters, relationships, or problems? • What are you noticing about how they are changing or what they are learning? • *What else are you noticing, thinking, or wondering?*

End	• What do you think about the way this book ended?
	• Thinking back across the book . . .
	  - what are some big ways the character seemed to change?
	  - what are some big lessons the character seemed to learn?
	• What big ideas do you think this book wanted us to consider? What do you think the author might have wanted us to learn, think about, or understand?

(continues)

Figure 7.1 *Continued*

RST

Beginning	*All of the previous in N–Q and . . .* • What are you noticing, learning, or wondering about this time and place? *What else?* • What are you noticing, learning, or wondering about the characters? *What else?* • What big ideas or themes do you think this book might address? *What else?* • What questions are you carrying? *This is a big one. As books become more challenging, we are going to have more questions that aren't answered for us right away. So instead of tossing the book aside because it's too hard or confusing, sometimes kids need practice naming and holding onto their questions. Kids need to know it's OK to live with ambiguity, to have questions and confusion in complicated books. They should keep reading and expect to learn and understand more as they go.*

Middle/ As You Read	*All of the previous in N–Q and . . .*
	
	• What *else* are you noticing, learning, or wondering about . . .
	  - the characters?
	  - the relationships?
	  - this time and place?
	• What are you noticing about how the different pieces of the story are fitting together?
	• Why do you think the author keeps repeating that word or phrase, referring to that object, or having the character do that particular thing?
	
	In the RST band and above, there are likely more small details that hold significance or that contain layers of meaning than before.
	
	• What are you noticing about this minor character? How do you think he/she is going to fit inside this story?

End	*All of the previous in N–Q and . . .* • What do you think the author wanted us to learn or think about this topic/setting/story? • What new questions or ideas do you have about this topic/setting/ character/story?

Figure 7.1 *Continued*

U V W and above

All of the previous in N–T and . . .

Beginning

- What are you noticing about the way the author is structuring this book/text? Why do you think she made those choices?

Books at levels UVW are often unpredictably structured and there is no simple organizing factor that kids can always lean on. We have to pay careful attention to the author's choices and craft decisions because the structure (as is true in all books!) is intentional and affects our experience/understanding of the book.

- What do you think this author's stance is likely to be about a particular big issue?

All of the previous in N–T and . . .

Middle/ As You Read

- What new information are you learning about the big issues that are at the heart of this book?
- What are you noticing about how the different threads/stories/perspectives fit together or conflict with one another?

All of the previous in N–T and . . .

End

- What new ideas are you growing about the issues or topics addressed inside this book?
- What new thoughts, questions, or opinions do you have about the issues/topics/ideas embedded in this book?
- How did this book change or affect you?

While any book can change us at any time, the books at levels UVW are almost always dealing with more profound, often painful, themes and topics. These books are often the ones that change the way kids see the world around them and begin to imagine themselves as actors in it.

Once we've made our way through more text, I might give a bit more time during the turn-and-talks because we have built a foundation and have more to work with. And for those moments in which I choose to have a whole-class conversation, we aim to make the exchange of ideas substantive and worthwhile. Most importantly, however, I don't end every turn-and-talk with a share-out of ideas; I choose very carefully when that happens. If I had them share every time, it would slow down the momentum of our reading together *and* imply that I was looking for right answers. Instead I am holding them all accountable to the work of thinking. And I'm listening in to what they are saying because it gives me so much information about who they are as thinkers and what support they might need in their independent reading lives.

Tip 14: Listen to Yourself

Benjamin Zander, conductor of the Boston Philharmonic Orchestra and the Boston Philharmonic Youth Orchestra, spoke about leading large groups of musicians and the transformative power of music in our lives. One thing he said stood out, especially as it relates to leading discussions about the books we read with kids: "The conductor doesn't make a sound. He depends for his power on his ability to make other people powerful. I realized my job was to awaken possibility in other people" (2017). I can't imagine a more beautiful job description. We are conductors too. When we invite children to talk about their ideas, we are empowering them to reach for understanding, dig a little deeper, or consider a new point of view. In order to do this well, we have to make sure the words we use, and the way we use them, awaken possibility.

I'm sure you've heard the common expression "It's not *what* you say; it's *how* you say it." In this context it's particularly true. The question "So what do you think about this character so far?" can lead to completely different conversations depending on the tone of your voice. I always make sure to ask any question with genuine sincerity, to indicate to kids I truly want to know what they think! The difference between "What are you noticing so far about Opal?" and "What are the most important character traits we've learned so far about Opal?" is even more significant, however. It feels a bit like the difference between my instructor at the Met asking, "What do you notice about the painting?" and "What are the most important elements of this painting?" The first awakens possibility, empowers students to come up with their own observations, and holds them accountable for noticing. The second sends an implicit message that *we* hold the power, and their access to power is the result of answering our question right. In the same way the majesty of Jackson Pollock's painting didn't belong to my Lincoln Center instructor, the artistry of a piece of children's literature doesn't belong to me.

Whenever we read a book or get started on an inquiry, we don't go in knowing all the answers yet. We open a book and expect to learn, to discover, to grow new insights and knowledge. Sometimes it takes a few chapters to get a full sense of who the characters are and the world they inhabit. Sometimes we get to the end of the book and realize our first impressions were completely off. When we begin a book, especially one that is more complicated, we need to read with a flexible, open stance, and kids need practice with reading and thinking in this way.

Opening up your questions can be as simple as integrating a few key words into your repertoire. My go-to words are pretty simple but they shift the dynamics in significant ways. They are *think*, *might*, and *seem*. Three tiny words, but they really do the trick! When I incorporate those words in my questions, I begin to open up what's possible. According to Webster's dictionary, *might* is a word that is "used to say that something is possible" and *seem* is defined as "to appear to the observation or understanding." Isn't that exactly what we are doing as we read? We are looking closely at what *appears* to be true, but we aren't totally sure yet until we continue to read and learn. We are trying to figure out what characters *might* be like and what they *appear* to be motivated by. The point is, we want to invite kids to wrestle, to inquire, to think, and to revise.

Questions That Awaken Possibility

What are you noticing about this character? How *might* you describe her? Turn and talk.

What do you *think* about this character? What kind of character does she *seem* to be?

Why do you *think* the character *might* have done that?

What do you *think might* be going on here?

Why do you *think* the author *might* have written it this way [started this way, ended this way, included this here]?

What *seems* to be the most important information to hold onto here? What do you *think* we should hold onto before heading into a new chapter?

What are you noticing about this picture? Why do you *think* the illustrator drew it this way? What do you *think* he might be trying to show us or get us to think about?

We also have to monitor how much airtime we give ourselves as we facilitate conversation. Are we dominating the airwaves or are the kids' voices the major players? It is essential to let kids make the music and do the talking and thinking, especially in whole-group conversations. Like conductors, we can do so much communicating without ever making a sound. I try hard to use my silent, expressive face to indicate how impressed I am by the turn taking, the new idea, or the passionate discourse. My face lights up, smiles, or gives an astonished look. I also show that I'm honoring and considering a child's words by nodding and almost looking up into my brain.

When group conversations begin to take root in your classroom, lots of kids will still look only in *your* eyes when they speak—as though, again, it's all about pleasing you. I encourage them to look at their classmates by silently circling my finger around, pointing to the whole group. I sometimes even break eye contact. I've also known teachers who purposefully removed themselves from conversations, sometimes whispering or physicalizing encouragement to a child who was reluctant to express his or her idea, sometimes recording or typing the conversation in order to reflect on the transcript later. All of these practices hold kids accountable to sustaining the conversation on their own and get them out of the habit of looking at us for validation.

Tip 15: Model and Teach Powerful Listening

One of the reasons why I believe so strongly in the read-aloud is because it carves out a space every day for kids to practice listening, an essential skill. This is a time when conversations are fever-pitched, when the loudest voices are the ones that get the most airtime, when people are all too often closed off to any other point of view. Perhaps that has always been true, but it feels particularly true now.

Not only does read-aloud require children to listen to text with fully activated minds and senses, but it also asks children to listen to *each other*—to turn toward each other and look one another in the eyes. This is no small thing. And children need practice doing it. We look at one another and listen to one another less and less these days. We look down more than we look up, and we interact more with our devices than with each other. Sherry Turkle writes, "Not too long ago, people walked with their heads up, looking at the water, the trees, the sky, and at one another talking. Now they often walk with their heads down, typing. Even when they are with friends, partners, or children, everyone is on their own devices. So, I say, look up, look at one another, and let's start a conversation" (2012).

During read-aloud, you model what powerful listening looks and feels like. When kids are turning and talking, having small-group or whole-class conversations, you can model and demonstrate listening. You can get down on the rug, or right up close to a partnership, and listen in, demonstrating your interest by being fully present, looking between each child, and honoring their words without saying a thing. You can demonstrate how a powerful listener responds to what she is hearing by repeating back what a child says, instead of just moving on to something else, which is a conversation move people often forget to do. You can ask a partnership or a small group to share out what they said to the whole group and let kids listen to their wise ideas, while at the same time demonstrating what really listening looks like—by looking closely at the person sharing, nodding your head, and taking his words seriously. When a partnership or small group shares, I often follow up with a simple question: "What do you all think about that?" or "How does that idea fit with what you were saying? Turn and talk."

Check out Video 5 for some examples of powerful listening in action.

Video 5
Genuinely
Listening
to Support
Conversation

See p. ix on how to access this video clip and others found in the book.

Modeling Active Listening

1. Get in close with partnerships when they are turning and talking. Pull up a chair, crouch down close to them, huddle with them on the rug. Listen in without saying anything.

2. After a child offers an idea, resist the urge to fill the space with your voice. Instead, try the following: just nod your head, say, "Hmm," like you are really mulling over the words, or invite her to say more.

3. Repeat back exactly what a child said, echoing the words to show you are truly taking them in. This communicates to the child your belief that her words are valuable and full of possibility.

Active listening is not just about sitting quietly while another person speaks—that's just being quiet. Sometimes even in conversations among adults, we are just waiting for our turn to speak. This is something you can actively work on during read-aloud conversations. You might say, "As we turn and talk today [or have a whole-group conversation], pay attention to the kind of conversationalist you are being. Are you listening enough? Are you trying to grow an idea with your friends, or are you just waiting to throw out one of your own? Do you need to push yourself to say a bit more or take a risk with a thought or idea? Today make sure you check in with yourself about the kind of conversationalist and listener you are being."

When we practice and engage in real listening, we are doing more than modeling and teaching one of the most important human skills we can teach children; we are also learning so much more about who is right in front of us. Our listening leads to greater understanding of what kinds of thinkers, readers, and learners live in our rooms, and it helps us teach them better all day long.

8

Principle Six

Take a Breath

Slowing down, lingering, and living inside the moment

When we pause, allow a gap and breathe deeply, we can experience instant refreshment. Suddenly, we slow down, look out, and there's the world.
—PEMA CHÖDRÖN

Everyone I know is busy. Even when we go on vacation, I find myself itching to check my phone to see what new alerts are there. I think I sometimes have fooled myself into thinking that the busier I am, the more important I must be. But deep down I know that's not true. In the words of *On Being* columnist Omid Safi, "How did we end up living like this? Why do we do this to ourselves? Why do we do this to our children? When did we forget that we are human beings, not human doings?" (2014).

This is something I am working on, as a person and a friend, definitely as a mom, and always as a teacher. I don't ever recall a single moment as a classroom teacher when I finished for the day and thought to myself, "Nothing more I could do here! Every box checked." As far as I'm concerned, there is no one busier than a teacher. And there is an urgency to teaching that is real and valid, because there really is *so much to do* in such a precious amount of time. But I think way too many of us are living and working at a pace that sometimes feels impossible to sustain.

That brings us to the point of this chapter: We all need to take a breath. We need it, the kids need it, our classrooms need it, and our world needs it. Many schools are launching meditation or mindfulness initiatives in order to promote well-being and de-escalate stress and anxiety in kids. I wonder what an impact a daily dose of mindfulness would have had on my kids and me. I imagine it would have been a powerful tool but I never tried it. I did, however, create moments of silence and opportunities to breathe and slow down. Every day, my students and I had a chance to take a breath because no matter what, I always read aloud to them.

My friend Charlie Alterman, a longtime Broadway musical director, says one of the most important elements of his job is keeping the orchestra in sync and making sure musicians don't get ahead of themselves, especially during a particularly riveting or fast-paced part of a score, or over the course of a long running show. This is true for singers too. Singers can't rush through an aria or a complicated string of notes. They have to stay connected to the breath and sing through each note, without skimming over or giving short shrift to a phrase or musical passage. When musicians rush, the whole thing can fall apart. Sound familiar? The time we spend reading aloud is a chance to slow down and create a space for meaningful listening and learning that doesn't depend on any bells and whistles.

Tip 16: Slow Down Key Words and Parts

I am a fast talker. My mom laughs that my grandfather claimed he never understood a word I said from the minute I started talking. Whenever I told a story, he would look around the table with a befuddled expression that seemed to say, "Is she for real? Can anyone actually understand what she is saying!?" So when I read aloud, I need to be aware of my pacing. Slowing down in an overly exaggerated way can end up feeling false, even condescending, to kids. But there are times when I need to put on the brakes and read in a very intentional, careful way. I try to enjoy the words and give them their due, especially when something significant is happening in the book or an important piece of information is being revealed. The most important thing to remember is not to read every single line of text slowly, but to read mindfully, with an ear and eye for key passages or places in the text.

Times and Places to Slow Your Reading Down

1. *Most informational or nonfiction texts*, especially when you are just getting started in a unit of study or inquiry project. That kind of reading is often slower. You are building knowledge brick by brick and often have to pause to ask, "How does this fit with what I already know?" or "What new information am I learning?"

    I often model the way readers read a chunk of nonfiction and then pause to check in for understanding using the following strategy:

    1. *Read a solid chunk. Pause.*
    2. *Ask myself, "Were there any patterns? Words or phrases that were repeated? What does that make me think?"*
    3. *Go back and look over paragraphs. Try to remember and retell the chunk using words from the text and my own.*
    4. *Check in: "Do I get it? Does it make sense?"*

2. *Books at lower Guided Reading levels.* I tend to read books through level L more slowly than books at levels M and above to encourage and enable kids to look closely and take in both the text and the illustrations, especially because they are often younger at these levels.

3. *Picture books.* It's important to give kids time to absorb the often-gorgeous language of picture books. But it's also important that we practice studying the pictures—taking note of the choices the illustrator has made to convey important ideas and feelings.

4. *Poems and books that are written in verse.* I almost always find myself reading slower throughout poetry and lyrical books, such as *Out of the Dust* (Hesse 1999), *Inside Out and Back Again* (Lai 2013), and Jacqueline Woodson's *Brown Girl Dreaming* (2014).

5. *Unfamiliar or tricky vocabulary.* When I come across tricky vocabulary or unknown words, I always put on the brakes a bit and read the word with emphasis, often using embodiment or gesture to convey meaning.

6. *Moments of emotional significance.* The stakes are often high in children's books—characters are dealing with great losses, embarking upon epic journeys both external and internal, and learning to accept difficult realities or painful truths. I always make sure to slow emotional moments down so kids can think about the literary elements and process big feelings as well.

7. *Moments when a character experiences a significant revelation or discovery.* These kinds of moments tend to happen once you get going in the book, but be on the lookout for seeds the author plants at the very beginning because they are often connected to a big reveal later on in the book.

8. *Moments of suspense.* Often, authors will slow down the text for you during moments of suspense by drawing out the action, using one-word sentences, and building tension.

9. *Beginnings of books.* Getting started in a new book can be a challenge, especially as books become more complicated. It's important to slow down enough to keep track and develop a feel for the characters, the details of the setting, the voice, and the structure of a book. Taking time in the beginning makes it possible to crank up your speed later on, once you have a strong sense for the new world you are bringing to life in your mind. (More on this in Chapter 4.)

10. *Endings of chapters.* Authors end chapters with intention. It's important to honor the closing lines, and pause to think about what has come before and what might be coming next. This gets kids ready to do the important work of synthesizing, determining importance, predicting, and talking together about what they are noticing.

11. *Endings of books.* There is nothing sweeter than that moment after you finish the last word of a book you have spent weeks reading aloud together. Take your time! Let yourself dwell for a second in that well-deserved full-circle moment.

When we vary our pacing and lean into certain passages, we communicate that real readers read at different paces depending upon the nature of the text or the significance of the moment. We make clear that strong readers shift gears emotionally and mentally. If we don't teach kids how, when, or why it pays off to slow down, lots of kids just read their books in order to get to the finish line. Some kids even get the idea that reading fast is a badge of honor, especially because we sometimes send a message that the point of reading is to get through as many books as possible instead of deeply understanding or thinking about them (think of any reading contest that gives rewards for reading the most books). And reading short texts quickly and efficiently is often valued as part of a strong test taker's battery of skills.

Other kids are "plot junkies" (a fabulous term I heard Mary Ehrenworth use at Teachers College once), speeding through books in search of the action, the resolution, the way things work out in the end. These kids miss stuff. A lot of stuff sometimes. And this affects their comprehension in serious ways.

As you read, be on the lookout for places where it seems the author is asking you to slow down. The following section of *Number the Stars* (Lowry 1989) is a good example of a place that requires reading with a sense of gravity and intentionally slow pacing. In this moment, main character Annemarie's best friend, Ellen, and her family are preparing to leave behind their old life in Denmark to escape to Sweden during World War II. Annemarie is thinking about what it means to have pride after losing so much and leaving behind so much of who they were.

> *All of those things, those sources of pride—the candlesticks, the books, the daydreams of theater—had been left behind in Copenhagen. They had nothing with them now; there was only the clothing of unknown people for warmth, the food from Henrik's farm for survival, and the dark path ahead, through the woods, to freedom.*
>
> *Annemarie realized, though she had not really been told, that Uncle Henrik was going to take them, in his boat, across the sea to Sweden. She knew how frightened Mrs. Rosen was of the sea: its width, its depth, its cold. She knew how frightened Ellen was of the soldiers, with their guns and boots, who were certainly looking for them. And she knew how frightened they all must be of the future.*
>
> *But their shoulders were as straight as they had been in the past: in the classroom, on the stage, at the Sabbath table. So there were other sources, too, of pride, and they had not left everything behind. (94)*

Every word in this passage feels significant. There are certain nameable qualities of this writing that make it almost impossible not to slow down so that when you read aloud, kids can absorb the power of this writing and this moment in the story:

- *The naming of so many different objects in a short passage.* Each object creates a strong image with powerful associations: candlesticks, books, clothing of unknown people, and more. I want to make sure each object or image is heard clearly, almost punctuated on its own, because each one feels like a symbol of something larger.

- *The repeated use of the phrase "She knew."* When phrases are repeated, it can begin to feel more like poetry than prose, which always slows me down. Repetition is also a signal to the reader that this is a moment that demands attention.

- *The moment of realization or discovery for Annemarie.* When characters come to an important realization, readers know to lean in. What is this character realizing and why is that important? What might this author be trying to teach us in this part? How might this realization be connected to the big ideas or themes in this book?

- *The description of something painful.* This is a moment about people on a long and treacherous journey, who have left their homes and are fleeing for survival. There are lots of painful moments in books, and I think kids are often yearning to have adults name for them the realities of suffering they know exist in the world. When I slow down a painful moment, it communicates to kids that I am not afraid to walk through that fire with them, that I'm not going to smooth it over or rush through it. I want to show them that we have to honor the difficulties and losses that all of us go through, whether the people going through it are fictional or not.

For examples of moments when I deliberately slow down and vary my pacing, take a look at Video 6.

The places where you slow the pace in read-aloud are places you might return to in writing workshop. We often tell young writers to slow down the most important moments of their stories by including every small action or part, which is exactly what Gaia Cornwell does in the wonderful picture book *Jabari Jumps*

Video 6
Slowing Down with Intention

See p. ix on how to access this video clip and others found in the book.

(2017), a story of a young boy and his dad at the swimming pool. Jabari decides he wants to jump off the diving board but finds himself a little nervous. After dad's loving, patient support, Jabari decides he is ready.

> *He walked all the way to the end. . . .*
> *His toes curled around the rough edge.*
> *Jabari looked out, as far as he could see. He felt like he was ready.*
> *"I love surprises," he whispered.*
> *He took a deep breath and spread his arms and bent his knees.*

Reading certain passages slowly and with intention sets kids up to take in the writing and appreciate the deliberate choices an author has made. When they return to their own writing, these passages can serve as mentor texts for writing scenes with precision and power themselves.

Tip 17: Give Thinking More Time

One of the most common conversations I have with teachers is about time. There just never seems to be enough of it! Figuring out how to manage our time and make the most of our days can be daunting and often very stressful! How do we make time for kids to go deep and not just skim the surface? Even though our days are jam-packed, learning shouldn't feel frantic.

Two of my favorite phrases to use throughout my read-alouds are "Check in with yourself" and "Think silently in your own minds," which begs the question, doesn't all thinking take place in one's mind? But as we know, kids often like to think out loud, and this is a good reminder that we are not exploding into conversation, but staying quiet and internal for a moment before talking to each other. Before I prompt them with a turn-and-talk or whole-group question, I often say one of these phrases slowly, carefully, in a way that feels like shifting gears. That little pause before the conversation is important. It offers a space between the reading and the talking and it provides a transition while kids consider what they might share or talk through with their partner.

Sometimes, however, I ask kids to check in with themselves *instead* of inviting them to turn and talk. This can save time and help us get through more text. It also helps them remember that readers are always pausing to reflect and makes the turn-and-talks we do have even more productive and dynamic.

Prompts That Create a Space for Internal Thinking

- Check in with yourself about the picture you have in your mind right now. [*Pause.*] Can you see the scene, character, or moment in your brain clearly?

- Check in with yourself about what you are learning, wondering, or thinking right now. [*Pause.*] What new ideas, thoughts, or questions do you have?

- Think in your mind about what just happened. [*Pause.*] How does this fit with what you already know?

- Think in your minds about why the author might have chosen to use the word _____ here. [*Pause.*] Let's reread that part, and as you listen again, think about why the author might have chosen that word or written it that way.

- Think in your minds about what details we have just learned about this setting, or place and time. [*Pause.*] What ideas are you starting to get about this place?

If you choose to stop in order to talk, reflect, or even jot, it's presumably an important moment in the text, and kids are likely leaning in. They are ready and willing to do some thinking, so you are well positioned to take that second or two for quiet reflection. I always take advantage of those moments when kids are sucked into the read-aloud experience. When I have their complete attention and the room is quiet and focused, I don't rush the invitation to think. I take a breath and shift into thinking and talking mode. That small moment really does make a difference. It settles the room and sends a message that you are not rushed, this time matters, and that thinking is valuable. Even if you are feeling rushed, try to let this be real moment of thinking and not a forced one. Otherwise, we probably should have just gone to P.E. in the first place!

I use a few key phrases to help kids deepen their thinking and give the time that thinking needs and deserves. Whether I'm listening in to a partnership talk or a child offering an idea to the whole class, and the speaker comes to a stop, I often say simply, "Can you say more about that?" or even more directly, "Say more about that. What else goes with that idea?" Then I wait with an expression that says, "I've got nowhere else in the world to be right now except right here with you, and I'm patient and eager to hear your ideas." More than anything, I think kids (and all humans, really) crave that experience of someone really listening to their ideas, even if it takes a minute to figure out exactly what they are trying to say, so we can't rush these moments. Video 7 shows (a few) moments when I give students time to think, when I try to linger a bit with them as they mull something over.

Another key reason to give thinking more time is that our first stab at anything isn't usually our best work. Creating something beautiful—a painting, a poem, even a well-crafted thought—takes time and reflection. It's not easy or comfortable to dwell in uncertainty, to stay in the struggle. It can also be similarly uncomfortable to take that extra minute of silence to allow a stronger thought to emerge or take root in our classrooms. And it's often doubly uncomfortable for us because we feel so pressed for time.

But integrating moments of silence into our daily practice is critical. Tina Chang, a classmate and friend of Poet Laureate Tracy K. Smith, described how Smith would allow everyone else in the circle to speak, listening carefully to their comments, before she took her turn. "That's a lot of where her wisdom came from, the value of silence and pause," said Chang (Franklin 2018). As a classroom teacher, it can be difficult to resist the urge to move quickly from thing to thing, child to child. But when we give children time to think, when we integrate moments of silence into our practice, we all notice more deeply. That is what helps us become wise.

Video 7
Giving Time to Think

See p. ix on how to access this video clip and others found in the book.

Tip 18: Remember the Power of the Pause

On my last trip back to New York City, there was one Broadway show that I knew I had to see: a new musical called *The Band's Visit*. I knew there must be something unusual about this show because it had won ten Tony Awards, more than *A Chorus Line*, *The Lion King*, and *Les Misérables* even though it had none of the razzle-dazzle or name recognition that those shows and most blockbuster Broadway musicals usually have. *The Band's Visit* is based on a little-known independent Israeli film, runs just over ninety minutes, and is set in a place that most people have never heard of. Why were people flocking to see this show? Why was it having such a profound impact?

Aside from the gorgeous music and performances, I think the show struck a chord with people because it was quiet, it was genuine, and it was *slow*. Orin Wolf, lead producer of *The Band's Visit*, said, "The world is getting louder and faster and funnier, and Broadway musicals—even the very artistic shows—are getting louder and louder, but my show doesn't subscribe to that" (Paulson 2018). It's true, *The Band's Visit* was one of the slower and quieter shows I've ever seen. There were long silences between the characters, and the transitions between scenes weren't snappy or an attempt to fill the space. I think we are so accustomed to living in a world with constant input, where nothing ever stops and no moment is left unfilled, that it was a profound relief to watch this musical quietly, gently unfold. It was a revelation.

While the show was quiet and slow, it was also aesthetically beautiful: the lighting, the instrumentation, the exquisite voices of the performers. We do not teach in rooms with gorgeous lighting or scenery. Like many of you, I've taught in hundreds of different rooms—in basements, in trailers in parking lots, in tiny, hot spaces and huge rooms that lack intimacy or anything close to loveliness. Despite all that, we can still create moments of staggering beauty.

No matter where you teach, when you honor the words of a book, when you create moments of stillness, when you slow down passages in books that take your breath away and allow the words to come alive, you are able to transcend the external circumstances of your classroom and experience something truly memorable and artistic. Those tiny beats can make a world of difference. There is beauty and possibility in the pause. Poet and writer Naomi Shihab Nye describes it this way:

I have always loved the gaps, the spaces between things, as much as the things. I love staring, pondering, mulling, puttering. I love the times when someone or something is late—there's that rich possibility of noticing more, in the meantime. . . . Poetry calls us to pause. There is so much we overlook, while the abundance around us continues to shimmer, on its own.

Video 8

The Power of the Pause in Fourth Grade

Video 9

The Power of the Pause in Seventh Grade

See p. ix on how to access these video clips and others found in the book.

For our purposes, I might add *read-aloud* calls us to pause. When we rush, we have the tendency to overlook. When we allow the story or text, the words or ideas, to linger or hang in the air a bit before doing anything next, we create a space for the "abundance around us . . . to shimmer, on its own." That shimmering is the intangible magic that fills the silence, making the moment feel rich with meaning and significance. It's what I think a lot of people responded to when they watched *The Band's Visit*, with all its silences and spaces between things. Check out some examples of those tiny yet significant beats in Videos 8 and 9.

So much depends on the power of the pause, that little moment of intention before and after and in between. Try it out. When you pause the read-aloud to think aloud or invite conversation, take just a beat longer before saying anything. When you get ready to start your reading for the day, remember the power of the pause and take a breath before you start. When you shift from talking back into reading again, remember the pause. There is ceremony in the pause; there is a crackle of anticipation. Things sift and settle and shake themselves out in that still moment. It's not long, barely two or three seconds. But it creates a sense of focus, presence, and togetherness in the moment. We are all longing for those moments, and kids more than ever, I think. Reading aloud helps us find moments to practice the art of not rushing and instead to engage deeply, to slow down, to pause and take a breath.

9

Principle Seven

Be Awed

Loving up the words and modeling your passion

Beauty is that in the presence of which we feel more alive.
—PHILOSOPHER AND POET JOHN O'DONOHUE

I love children's books. I love them so much that I can spend hours looking at the children's section in bookstores or libraries. I love the quirky, plucky characters and the ones that break your heart with their passion, determination, and grit—the way they persevere and struggle through sorrows, disappointments, and despair. I love the gorgeous (and sometimes hilarious) illustrations in picture books and on the covers of young adult novels. I love the sweetness and sense of possibility inside so many of them—the ways characters learn lessons about friendship and teamwork, making the world a better place, and how to fight against unfairness and injustice. I love the authors who are telling the stories of our kids and our world in ways that are empowering a new generation of readers and citizens. A well-written children's book is one of life's greatest gifts.

I make no bones about this love with students, and I nurture it because I know that it feeds not only me but them. The first thing on the Teachers College Reading and Writing Project's Bill of Rights for Reading and Writing is "Above all, good teachers matter. Learners need teachers who demonstrate what it means to live richly literate lives, wearing a love of reading and writing on their sleeves." I want to show my students that books can help them cast aside the weight of this difficult world, make it possible to hope and dream, and give them a road map for navigating the challenges of growing up and being citizens of this world. I want children to fall in love with reading because I know it can save their lives.

There are plenty of people who would echo this idea, but one of the most powerful declarations I've come across was written by Kevin Powers, an Iraq War veteran, novelist, and poet who struggled with depression and addiction following his term in Iraq:

> *Books saved my life. Those four words seem absurd. And yet I believe them to be true as much as or more than I believe anything else that I can't prove. . . . I recognized myself in another, and somehow that simple tether allowed me to slowly pull myself away from one of the most terrifying beliefs common to the kind of ailment I'm describing: that one is utterly alone, uniquely so, and that this condition is permanent. (2018)*

Books, like so many great works of art, can reach across the space and make us feel less alone and more connected to the full range of human experience. I don't want kids to miss out on the limitless, transcendent potential of reading because we spend all our time focusing on the mechanics, the skills of comprehension in isolation, or diligent critical analysis (all of which matter, of course, but as part of a balanced literacy diet). Artists pursue their creative careers because they love what they do and feel passionate about their work. We are no different. Wearing our love of literature and books on our sleeve is more than just personal preference; it is actually an essential part of our practice.

Tip 19: Dazzle First

Anyone who knows anything about musicals knows that they often begin with a grand opening number that pulls out all the stops. There are just too many brilliant ones to name here, but *The Ballad of Sweeney Todd* might top my list of favorites. It comes at you like an orchestral freight train and leaves no doubt that you are about to have a bona fide theatrical experience. Lots of musicals do this: they dazzle first and leave you wanting more. This is precisely what we do when we read aloud! We have to get students excited about reading because it will leave them wanting more and help them stay motivated for the hard work that reading requires.

Nothing can do the work of dazzling students more effectively than a great text. Almost all my best ideas and lesson plans hinge on the selection of a great text that leads the way, that inspires questions or conversations or an enthusiastic, emotional response. A great text does so much of the work for me! I don't need to convince the kids that they are about to embark on some exciting new curricular journey. More than anything, I need to engage them in the experience by going straight to the heart of the thing. Basically, I need an opening number. In an interview about the importance of teachers, student engagement, and the power of poetry, Cornelius Minor asked Newbery Award–winning author and poet Kwame Alexander about his "go-to strategy" for engaging kids right from the start in his writing workshops. He replied that his tip was to *show* what poetry is—the playfulness of words, the visceral punch of poetry, and the power of story. Alexander often starts a workshop by walking in and just reading a poem right away, not even introducing himself, just bringing "the words from the page onto the stage" (Alexander 2018). By showing kids that poetry is cool instead of telling them, he pulls them in. He is communicating to them that "I've got you. You're into it. What's next?" (Alexander 2018).

All of us can lean on books to pique kids' interest, to get their eyes up and their hearts open, to make them laugh and feel moved. All of us can dazzle kids by giving them wholly immersive experiences in reading that can't be substituted with talk *about* reading or activities that are related to books and stories but that aren't connected to the work of real reading. We have to engage them with spectacular texts because, as Jen Serravallo writes, "without engagement, you've got nothing" (2015). The read-aloud is a tried-and-true tool for engaging students right away and providing an entry point for units of study across the curriculum.

One of the best ways to set the stage and to engage students right off the bat is with dazzling picture books. This is a particularly powerful tool with middle schoolers, who are often our most disengaged, dormant readers. As Pernille Ripp, middle school teacher and founder of the Global Read Aloud, says, "Picture books can make us feel successful when we have lost our way" (2015). Middle schoolers are often the most likely to feel they have lost their way with reading. Using a picture book to launch units in science, social studies, and other content areas is a perfect tool for igniting their interest and giving them some background knowledge right away with a book that includes gorgeous pictures and content-rich vocabulary. Here are some picture books that I have used to launch units of study across different curricular areas.

Social Studies

Immigration and Migration

One of the best, most important middle school books I have read in many years is *Refugee* (Gratz 2017), which tells the story of three children from three different time periods and continents seeking refuge. It is riveting, inspiring, and heartbreaking. It also requires a bit of work in the beginning to understand the context of each child's situation, in terms of the political unrest and the historical circumstances. Before jumping into that book, or any unit on immigration, migration, or displacement, I might read a few picture books to help students understand the context surrounding each story in this novel. The pictures, vocabulary, and compelling stories give students background knowledge and provide a starting point for questions and wonderings that will launch your classroom inquiry into this topic.

The Journey, by Francesca Sanna (2016)

Teacup, by Rebecca Young (2016)

Stepping Stones, by Margriet Ruurs (2016)

The Keeping Quilt, by Patricia Polacco (2001)

Exploration

I am not a fan of any units that ask kids to memorize the names and travels of the men who sailed across the Atlantic in search of the New World. However, I like to look at the way in which authors depict the different explorers as a way to learn about the age of exploration and develop a critical lens at the same time. One of my favorite picture books to read aloud and study is *Follow the Dream: The Story of Christopher Columbus* (Sís 1991). We consider why Sís might have written the book, what his point of view is, what he is trying to get us to think about Columbus. The second to last page, which shows a very small and unencumbered Christopher Columbus (no ships, no other men, no spears or flags) on the shore of a peaceful blue sea with a group of Native Americans standing in a semicircle on the shore, is a perfect illustration to linger over with kids. What do you notice about this illustration? What do you see? Why do you think Sís ended the story of Columbus this way? Why do you think he made the artistic and textual choices he did? What do you think Sís is trying to get us to think about Columbus here? And what do *you* think about that?

American Revolution

Colonial Voices: Hear Them Speak, by Kay Winters (2015)

George vs. George, by Rosalyn Schanzer (2007)

Independent Dames, by Laurie Halse Anderson (2008)

Science

Ecosystems and Oceanography

Coral Reef, by Jason Chin (2016)

Down, Down, Down: A Journey to the Bottom of the Sea, by Steve Jenkins (2009)

Wolf Island, by Celia Godkin (2006)

Evolution, Natural Selection, and Species

Island: A Story of the Galápagos, by Jason Chin (2012)

Any book by Jason Chin is a great starter for any unit of science. His pictures, text, and artistry are both fascinating and stunning. In fact, a middle school science teacher told me she had never seen an explanation of evolution so beautifully and clearly explained as it is in his book *Island*.

Geology and Earth Science

A Rock Is Lively (Aston 2015b) is a lovely book from the creators of the equally wonderful books *An Egg Is Quiet* (2014a), *A Seed Is Sleepy* (2014b), *A Butterfly Is Patient* (2015a), and *A Nest Is Noisy* (2017). What I love about these books is how much they honor both the subject matter and the reader. These books are not only chock-full of interesting information but also imaginative and beautiful without feeling precious, which make them terrific choices for both younger and older audiences. Upper-grade and middle school students are able to appreciate the artistry of these books and the sophisticated, well-designed presentation of the subject matter.

For some great interactive read-aloud lessons using picture books from Next Generation Science Standards for grades K–5, go to www.kbs.msu.edu/wp-content/uploads/2017/02/NGSS-Interactive-Read-Alouds.pdf.

Middle School ELA Units

Using picture books to teach literary concepts or launch any number of units in both reading and writing is an often underutilized tool. It's a perfect way to teach and practice analyzing and annotating text, tracking character development, understanding unreliable narration, developing thematic statements, and learning from a writer's craft because you can do any one of those things in one sitting! All of these skills are sophisticated and kids benefit from opportunities to practice and gain confidence with this work using short, visually interesting books before launching into more difficult text. Not to mention the fact that picture books are often told in stunning, poetic language, and many of them address big issues that take much longer to unpack in novels. Even wordless picture books like JiHyeon Lee's *Pool* (2015) and *Door* (2018) help kids deepen their inferential thinking skills and can lead to conversations about extended metaphors and symbolism that make room for all kinds of ideas—without the pressure of citing text or being "right."

One of my favorite books to use for meaningful conversations about metaphor and symbolism is *The Rabbit Listened* (Doerrfeld 2018). It might not strike you as a book meant for older kids, as it is about a young child whose tower of bricks is toppled over by a flock of birds. Eventually, a cast of animal characters shows up one by one to presumably comfort him, all to no avail, as they are not really paying attention to what the little boy needs, which is simply for someone to just sit with him and listen. The flock of birds, however, could represent any unexpected storm or loss or event that is upending and makes you wonder how you'll ever begin again. The book also helps us consider how the animals represent the different characters in other books and even the people in our lives. What characters or people might be the Bear (the character in *A Rabbit Listened* who just wants to rage and growl and get angry)? Who is the Stork (he just wants to push things under the rug and pretend nothing has happened)? Who is the Rabbit—the one who really understands what another character needs and provides comfort?

Tip 20: Reread and Repeat

Have you ever listened to a song you loved and then thought, "I want to listen to that again right away"? When I come across music that just opens up my heart, my instinct is to press Repeat, Repeat, Repeat. This feeling is akin to reading a passage that breaks open something in our hearts or makes something click in our minds. When that happens, we often pause, go back, and read it again. We reread for a whole host of important reasons: to figure out what exactly we just read, think more about the words or information, hold onto the ideas being articulated, get something straight, or simply savor the words.

Rereading is at the heart of close reading, a practice that schools have embraced more than ever in this age of high-stakes tests. It's always been true that when we've read texts, we've been on the lookout for passages, sentences, or parts that were particularly instructive or had multiple layers of meaning. Such parts often require a second, even a third or more, reading—not because you are trying to get answers right on a test, but because that's just what readers do when they are building knowledge or resonating with the words on a page. As part of a balanced literacy curriculum, students often practice close reading with short passages that are read multiple times during a shared reading lesson or in small groups, often with the intention of finding evidence or correct answers to questions. During the read-aloud, however, we have the chance to model the power and delight of rereading without any strings attached. We can show how certain passages inspire us to reread in order to uncover more layers or think again about the author's intentions, word choice, or craft. Acclaimed novelist Lauren Groff says, "The greatest texts, I think, first dazzle, then with careful rereading, they instruct" (Fassler 2015).

Here are some of the things I focus on when we reread:

1. *Vocabulary and new concepts.* Poet Dr. Elizabeth Alexander says, "Children are drawn toward language that shimmers, individual words with power. They will stop you and ask you to repeat a shimmering word if they're hearing it for the first time. You can see it in their faces" (2011). If we come across a word or phrase in the midst of a read-aloud, we might just repeat the word or reread the sentence. Repeating words that are "shimmering," informative, new, or important reinforces a love of language, reinforces new vocabulary

and concepts, and helps children begin to notice the creative, writerly choices an author has made. Sometimes I ask children to say the word with me and even attach a movement to the word in order to solidify its meaning. (See Figures 9.1 and 9.2.)

2. *Synthesis.* Sometimes, we go back to a passage and read it again with a different lens, perhaps after we make a discovery or a character makes an important realization or refers back to an earlier part in the book: "Let's go back to that part when _____ happened. Let's read that again and see if we notice any clues this time around that would have helped us predict what came next," or "Let's go back and

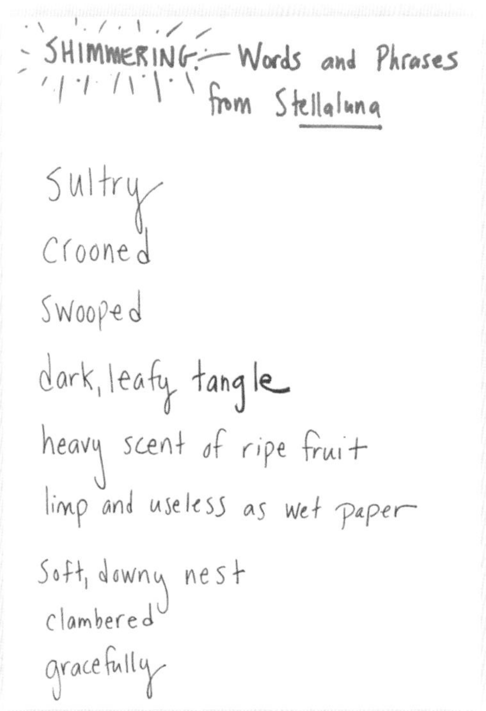

Figure 9.1 Shimmering Words Chart: *Stellaluna*

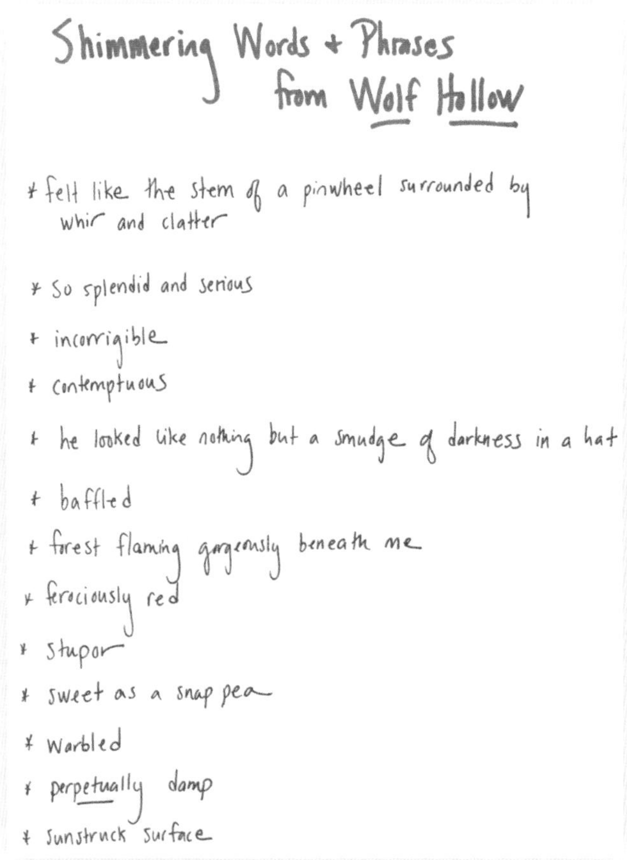

SHIMMERING Words and Phrases from Stellaluna

Sultry
Crooned
Swooped
dark, leafy tangle
heavy scent of ripe fruit
limp and useless as wet paper
Soft, downy nest
clambered
gracefully

Figure 9.2 Shimmering Words Chart: *Wolf Hollow*

Shimmering Words + Phrases from Wolf Hollow

* felt like the stem of a pinwheel surrounded by whir and clatter
* So splendid and serious
* incorrigible
* contemptuous
* he looked like nothing but a smudge of darkness in a hat
* baffled
* forest flaming gorgeously beneath me
* ferociously red
* stupor
* sweet as a snap pea
* warbled
* perpetually damp
* sunstruck surface

reread the beginning lines of this book and see what new things we notice now that we have finished the book."

3. *New information (monitoring for sense).* Sometimes I'll say, "Oh, let's read that again. My brain feels so full of important information. Let's be sure we didn't miss any important details or information there," or "That was chock-full of amazing information. Let's reread and make sure we keep that straight."

4. *Pure enjoyment of writer's craft.* I might say, "Wasn't that a gorgeous passage? That was too beautiful not to read again," or "Didn't that passage just stop you in your tracks? Let's reread that and think about the words the author used. What do you notice about the word choices she made?"

5. *Moments of significance.* "Wow. [*Pause.*] Let's read that part again. As we do, think again about why this moment is so important, why the character is saying [or doing] this. Think about what this brings to your mind and heart." Returning to a significant passage, page, or chapter of a read-aloud also makes a wonderful shared reading experience (or readers theatre experience; for more on that, see Chapter 11).

NOTICE MORE DEEPLY: Reasons to Pause & Reread

1) When you come across a delicious word or phrase. What makes it powerful or interesting? Take a second to linger, wonder, reread.

2) When something significant happens- a discovery, revelation, big feeling. Think back and reread the SEEDS the author planted leading up to that moment. What more do you notice?

3) When your brain feels chock-full of information. Pause and reread to make sure you didn't miss any important details or information.

4) When you read a part that SWEEPS you off your feet (like Lauren Wolk's description of the seasons in Wolf Hollow!). Read it again and enjoy the language and author's originality!

Figure 9.3 Reasons to Reread

Take a look in Video 10 at the way we both pause and reread a particularly beautiful part of Matt de la Peña's book *Last Stop on Market Street* (2015) in order to enjoy it and also consider the deeper meaning or message inside the book.

Video 10
Pause to Reread, Listen Again, and Discover More

See p. ix on how to access this video clip and others found in the book.

Tip 21: Express Your Love

After years away from show business, I found myself once again in a new musical called *October Sky* at the Old Globe Theatre in San Diego. I hadn't performed in a professional production for years and it was such an unexpected gift to be a part of a creative ensemble again and witness the adorable antics of a younger generation of performers. My part was tiny, which meant I had the chance to spend a lot of time watching other people learn their choreography, rehearse their scenes, and practice their songs. The musical is based on the true story of high school student Homer Hickham and his dream of launching a real rocket into space after seeing Sputnik fly across the sky in his small West Virginian hometown. With the help of three friends, he actually finds success—and ultimately becomes a NASA engineer. Every night, Kyle Selig (the actor playing Homer) and his buddies sang the song "Rocket Boys," where they made a pact to launch a rocket and show their hometown, and the world, what they could do against all odds. Those four young actors threw their heart into that song every night and we all watched them with big old grins our faces, every single time. At the end of the number, the guys would jump up on the set cafeteria table, throw their hands together to seal the deal, and pump them into the sky with jubilation. It was pure joy to watch and pure joy for them to perform.

Now, we can't exactly re-create this kind of scenario in the classroom, but we can find a way to tap into our delight about the books we read, because that delight is transmittable. In the same way that an audience feels a wave of energy when watching the Rocket Boys perform, we want our kids to watch us read and talk about books and think, "This reading thing is amazing! I want in!" More than anything, we want to show kids that we love books, reading, language, and stories. Here are some ways to show the love:

Ways to Express Our Love

1. Set up your library carefully and intentionally. Your classroom library is a physical representation of your love for books, so think about organizational systems that will make it inviting and accessible.

2. Talk about books and authors with your colleagues and let your kids observe the way books foster meaningful and ongoing connections and conversations.

3. Talk about the books you want to read and authors you are excited to get to know. Sharing your reading journey gives them a road map for embarking upon and sticking with their own.

4. Show your admiration for books by handling and displaying them with care.

5. Demonstrate interest in your children's reading lives by getting to know them as readers and checking in about book choices and reading goals. Check out Donalyn Miller's Reading Interest-a-Lyzer in *The Book Whisperer* (2009) for more information about this!

Loving up the books we read aloud, and the words that inhabit them, is an essential part of our practice. It does not belie a focus on rigor or quality instructional time. What we love is what we put our energy into; it is what motivates us to stay in the struggle or work hard to improve. We need our students to see that the reason we work hard on reading with stamina during independent reading time, or tackle genres that might not be our favorite, is because we *love* reading and the endless possibilities that books open up for us. The reason we annotate a dense passage or work hard to find evidence from the text in order to determine the big idea or author's purpose is because we want to get better at reading with power because there is nothing more satisfying than being swept away in a book we understand deeply. If kids don't see and experience this, they have no reason to buy into the idea that reading is worthwhile.

No one says it better than Chris Lehman and Kate Roberts, who write about loving words and reading in their book *Falling in Love with Close Reading* (2013). In their opening chapter, they remind us that making our love affair with the written word public helps students learn the importance of reading closely and reflecting in order to understand not only the text in front of us but also the world around and within us.

> *We know in our bones that loving something or someone involves knowing that thing or person very well. Returning to it repeatedly, gazing at it for hours, considering each angle, each word, and thinking about its meaning.*
>
> > *Our connection to the written word can be as deep as a love affair. . . . Love brings us in close, leads us to study the details of a thing, and asks us to return again and again. . . . Showing [students] how one word, one scene, or one idea matters . . . is an opportunity to extend a love affair with reading. It is also a*

chance to carry close reading habits beyond the page, to remind students that their lives are rich with significance, ready to be examined, reflected upon, and appreciated. (1–2)

Transmitting love of books is the antidote to disengaged readers, especially in middle and high school. So when we come upon a passage in a read-aloud that knocks our socks off, we must be willing to be astonished right there in front of thirty kids who may have never felt astonished by words before in their life. This doesn't mean taking on artificial enthusiasm or a voice that feels canned; find a way to take notice with your own brand of enthusiasm. Here are some things I tend to say when I come across a part I love:

"Wow! That was super interesting, wasn't it? I never knew that or thought about that in that way before!"

"That was such a beautiful passage, wasn't it? I just loved the way the author _____."

"Wow, can you believe [the character] finally came out and said that?! That was a pretty huge moment! It feels like we've been waiting the whole book for her to express those feelings."

"What an amazing way to express that idea! Did you hear how the author used the word _____ to express or show _____?"

"Wow. That was such a moving [hilarious, unexpected, touching, fascinating] passage."

It's important to model the way we pause and take notice—*it all hinges on how well we notice.* Readers miss key elements of a book when they don't know *how* to notice, what to pay attention to, or what it means to look closely. I think this may have to do with the frenetic pace of our lives these days, but looking closely is at the heart of it all. And that comes back to love. We look closely at things we love. We must remember, too, that our students are looking closely at us. They notice the moves we make, the things we love, the identities we nurture as readers and lovers of words. They pay attention to the ways in which we notice their reading moves and the kinds of books and topics they love, all of which affects the kinds of readers they become. In the words of the iconic Mister Rogers, "Love is at the root of everything, all learning, all parenting, all relationships. Love, or the lack of it" (Neville 2018).

It turns out that expressing our love during our daily read-alouds also has powerful benefits for our writing instruction. Lauren Groff says, "Our daily love of language can make writers out of people who never thought of themselves that way" (2015). By paying attention to what we love about the words we read, we will find ourselves with bountiful examples of strong, compelling writing. The mentor texts we choose fuel engagement for writing and give us a model for what expert writing sounds like. And the best way to use mentor texts in writing is to *notice first* what you loved about the writing! In fact, there's a pretty straightforward three-step process for using mentor texts to teach writing.

1. Notice first: What did the writer do in this piece that you liked (or loved!)? That you thought really worked?
2. Try to name what the writer did in terms of craft. What writerly thing did this author do? Try to name it in kid-friendly terms.
3. Once you've named it, try that writerly thing out in your own writing.

Renée Watson's book *Piecing Me Together* (2017) is a varied mix of longer prose and shorter chapters (one is only three lines long), some of which consist of a poetic list or just a single paragraph. The structure of the book reflects the way the main character, Jade, is piecing different parts of her identity together and learning to be and express her true self. Watson discussed how important it is to notice the craft and choices that authors make because they are intentional—they are a reflection of the writer's artistry and creativity. By paying attention to a writer's craft, you honor the work of that author and help children see themselves as creators who can make choices too.

So go to it: proudly declare your love affair with writing; allow yourself to be gobsmacked by the words you read. Be warned, however: you might just create a classroom full of not only readers but writers too!

10

Principle Eight

Dig Deep

Promoting equity, action, and change

Poetry is at the forefront of [social change], from the Declaration of
Independence to Martin Luther King's "I Have a Dream" speech. Poetry has
always been the thread that is weaving throughout . . . the fabric of American,
and global, history. . . . Words have the power to change the world both
locally and globally. And that realization is what inspires me every day.

—AMANDA GORMAN, FIRST YOUTH POET LAUREATE OF THE UNITED STATES

I believe that if you watched Youth Poet Laureate Amanda Gorman deliver her poetry (which is easy—just google it!), you, too, would be convinced that words have the power to change the world. In her poem "In This Place (An American Lyric)," Gorman reminds us that poems exist all throughout America, in its different cities and people. It's an ode to the diversity of America but also a rousing testament to the power of activism and civic engagement. Poems like Gorman's remind me why I have long been attracted— devoted even—to books, plays, the theatre, the classroom, and the work teachers do every day to empower young people to find and use their voices.

One of the most obvious ways to create a space for conversation about important issues relating to injustice, identity, power, and the abuse of power is to read books aloud that tackle those issues square on, and there are a lot of magnificent ones. I have my favorites, but it is critical to take the time to research the lists and book picks of organizations that are actively involved in the work of curating book lists for social justice or that reflect the experiences of underrepresented voices. I believe in prioritizing read-alouds that give students practice in listening to and learning from diverse voices, so I need to take time to listen and learn, with an open stance, about the books and voices that will teach me and my students.

Resources for Finding Diverse Books

- Teaching for Change: https://socialjusticebooks.org
- We Need Diverse Books: https://diversebooks.org
- Teaching Tolerance: www.teachingtolerance.org (This organization is committed to helping teachers "approach anti-bias, social justice and civil rights education" in a way that "makes complex topics easier to understand—and teach.")
- Lee and Low Books: https://blog.leeandlow.com/2014/05/22/checklist-8-steps -to-creating-a-diverse-book-collection/
- Project Lit Community: www.facebook.com/projectlitcommunity/

The books we include in our classroom libraries, and especially the books we choose to read aloud, communicate powerful messages about who and what we value. Reading aloud thoughtfully chosen books that center on social justice gives children opportunities to engage in meaningful conversation about current and historical issues and supports a curriculum dedicated to building more inclusive school communities. It also give kids the chance to practice the art of listening, which is an essential first step for pretty much everything: connecting with someone, understanding the experience or point of view of someone unlike yourself, reflecting on how you can make a difference, and taking steps to change your community or the world around you.

Tip 22: Question, Question, Question

In his 2017 TED talk, painter, sculptor, and MacArthur Genius Award winner Titus Kaphar speaks about the importance of shifting our gaze and noticing aspects of paintings or sculptures, and their accompanying historical significance, that often go unnoticed or unchallenged. He tells the story of taking his two sons to the American Museum of Natural History in New York City and approaching the main entrance, in front of which stands a large bronze sculpture of Teddy Roosevelt, who is riding on a horse, bold and strong. On the left-hand side of the sculpture, a Native American is walking, and on the right-hand side, an African American is walking. As they came closer to the sculpture, Kaphar's nine-year-old son slowed down to ask, "Dad, how come *he* gets to ride? And they have to walk?"

Kaphar says, "It stopped me in my tracks. . . . Fundamentally, what he was saying was, 'That doesn't look fair. . . . And why is this thing that's so not fair sitting outside such an amazing institution?' And his question got me wondering, is there a way for us to amend our public sculptures, our national monuments? Not *erase* them, but is there a way to amend them?" (2017). Kaphar goes on to teach about the importance of shifting our gaze, of centering the people in paintings that often go overlooked, such as the African American child in a seventeenth-century Fran Hals painting that depicts wealthy slave owners at the forefront. By painting over much of a replica of the painting (which Kaphar reproduced) with white paint and linseed oil, Kaphar demonstrates how the face of the young boy becomes the focal point of our gaze. As a result of the linseed oil, the faces of the other characters will begin to emerge, but with more muted colors and transparent tones. Kaphar's demonstration helps us think about how we can begin to notice things differently and pay attention to the hidden details or messages, so that we can begin to ask questions like, "Why do some have to walk?"

Book reading, like Kaphar's brilliant and perspective-shifting artwork, calls us to notice differently too, and it calls us to ask questions about fairness. Nathan Bowling, 2016 Washington Teacher of the Year, says, "Books, perhaps more than any other form of media, have the power to transform minds and perspectives. We'll never make real progress as a society unless we're able to broaden our horizons—that's the real power of books" (Bassett, Bigham, and Calvert 2017, 41). When we read aloud, we can create a space for students to engage in the same kinds of questioning that Kaphar describes. We can invite kids to wrestle with social justice issues or tackle challenging historical or contemporary concepts that keep kids in the reading game, help them feel empowered by books, and inspire them to think differently and perhaps even take action. Kids of all ages, but especially middle-grade kids, are chomping at the bit to learn and discuss real-world issues, regardless of their Lexile or Guided Reading level. All kids need access to these conversations. All kids need to feel they have a stake in building a world that reflects their hopes and dreams, that speaks to them, that tells them they can make a difference.

Perhaps the best way teachers can teach into social justice issues is not by having all the answers, but by teaching students to notice deeply and by making room for all the questions. When we read aloud, we can teach our students to pay close attention to the details inside a book, to think critically, to ask questions that might set them down a path of inquiry or light a fire of activism. In the words of James Baldwin, the artist "must drive to the heart of every answer and expose the question the answer hides." This is one of the great purposes of read-aloud too—to expose the questions hidden within the text.

When I read *Amal Unbound* (Saeed 2018) with a group of sixth and seventh graders, so much of our conversation was sparked by simply asking them to talk about what they noticed—about the characters, the seeds of "trouble," the themes and big issues the author seemed to be addressing, and the similarities and differences between this book and other books that deal with inequalities, bravery, power, injustice, and identity.

As we read, students tracked what they were noticing in order to prepare for turn-and-talks and longer conversations about the book. (See Figure 10.1.) Their jots were a huge source of data and reflection for me as well, and they were a way to engage with the students right away. "I see that you are noticing _____. Tell me more about why that stood out to you." For kids who wrote very little down, it helped me dig a little deeper. What else might they be attending to but not writing? Were they not writing down their noticings but still tracking the story? "I notice you wrote _____ down. Talk to me about what *else* you are noticing."

As I continued to read, we paid attention to the realities and limitations that Amal faced and what she did in response to them, always questioning and wondering along the way. At the end of the book, we thought about what the author's purpose might have been and what she might have been trying to teach her readers.

Figure 10.2 shows the questions I tend to ask as I read a book aloud, especially with upper-grade and middle school students. Sometimes I ask them to jot their thinking down in order to capture the invisible work their brains are doing, but most times, these are prompts for conversation.

notices	thinking/wonders
- there is a window	- Why does Amal like her teacher so much?
- person nararating has a sister	- is she gonna die?
- Amal's mom having a baby	- is the school going to explode or crash down?
- Amal can't write poety	- Parents going to die?
- She's at school	- why is Khan Sahib the center of "attention"?
- Amal has a best friend	- why does she have to meet omar? [Amal]
- Amal wants to know everything	- Why did Amal lie to her sister?
- Khan Sahib is the landlord	- will Khan Sahib be a problem later in time?
- Amal has a book from Omar	- will Omar spill some TE on Khan Sahib to Amal?
- Omar is a friend of Amal	- are they [Amals family] wealthy?
- Omar wants to be a lawyer	- does Amal want a friend thats a girl?
- Amals sister is 3-years-old	- why is Omal going to a new school

(the baby is coming)

Figure 10.1 Sixth Graders' Notes from the Beginning of *Amal Unbound*

Notice	Thinking
• The kids sister's uniform was a hand-me-down which was to big.	• Why is it Amals last day of school?
• Amal loved to stay after School.	• What is going to happen?
• Amal loves to read poetry	• Why did amal take life for granted?
• Amal remembers the smell of the chalkboard, taking life for granted in her last day of school.	• Why does the landlord or owner want to build a large building?
• Lives in Pakistan	• What does Omar have to say that is SO important?
• Amal wanted to know everything.	• Is Amals family wealthy?
• Khan Sahib seems to be excentrick and mean. He is blamed for everything Unusual.	• Why does the boys school have a bigger library than the girls school?
• Khan Sahib is a landlord.	
• Amal faked forgeting his test to hang out with her friend.	
• Amal most likely is going to be forced into work at the new building by her dad.	
• Amals mom doesn't want her to hang out with Omar because of gossip.	

Figure 10.2 Conversation Starters

What do you notice . . .

- about who has power here?
- about who has voice here?
- about who is front and center in this story/book and who is left out?
- about how this problem affects this character/ this community?
- about how this character feels about that?
- about how this character is treated?
- about how this character is acting?
- about how the other characters are reacting to this problem or character?
- about how the author describes this character?
- about the words used to describe this place/ problem?
- about how this author depicts this issue versus how you think or feel about this issue?
- about how the author ends this book/the way this book ends?
- about this illustration?
- about the choices the illustrator makes in this picture around color, size, shape, and focus?
- about how this book is making you feel?

What do you think about that?

What questions do you have about that?

Teaching our students to become strong readers is about more than just comprehension. It's about civic participation and the ability to engage in the discourse that shapes our community, our country, and our world. Jon Valant, education research fellow at the Brookings Institute, says,

> *Civic participation in 2018 is different from civic participation in 1950. Today, it's harder to instill empathy for people with different opinions because technology makes it easier to ignore those perspectives. You can unfriend someone on*

Facebook or mute specific phrases on Twitter. But living in a bubble means you have less opportunity or need to empathize with others. Plus, students are inundated with information from social media, and they need to learn how to wade through it all to find the facts. (Cardinali 2018)

We can use our read-alouds to model how readers, and citizens, pay attention, ask questions, listen well, and learn from people who have important stories to tell and whose work is rooted in strong research. We can have a shared conversation about the issues characters face, which leads us to think about our own choices and the issues that are important to us and our own communities.

One of things that I love most about reading a book aloud with any community is the potential to have conversations that call us to push past our first assumptions about any text we encounter together. How do we create a space for big conversations about complicated issues and make sure we pay attention to the voices of people who may have a very different life story or point of view? How do we safeguard our ability to stay open, to question without clinging to our own entrenched opinions, and find our way to a deeper or more nuanced understanding? In June of 2018, Dr. Atul Gawande gave the commencement address at UCLA's medical school and his words could easily be a commencement address to a group of graduating teachers:

Once we lose the desire to understand—to be surprised, to listen and bear witness—we lose our humanity. Among the most important capacities that you take with you today is your curiosity. You must guard it, for curiosity is the beginning of empathy. When others say that someone is evil or crazy, or even a hero or an angel, they are usually trying to shut off curiosity. Don't let them. We are all capable of heroic and of evil things. No one and nothing that you encounter in your life and career will be simply heroic or evil. Virtue is a capacity. It can always be lost or gained. That potential is why all of our lives are of equal worth. (Gawande 2018)

When we read books together, we are going to get into thorny territory sometimes. We are going to encounter characters who challenge our assumptions and authors who write from a particular, perhaps unfamiliar stance. It can be tricky to push past an impulse to write them off or judge them. But, as Dr. Gawande reminds us, we can't shut off our curiosity; we have to dig a little deeper. We have to ask ourselves, why would an author write a character this way? What might she have wanted us to wrestle with or consider? We have to make room for questions, even when we don't necessarily have perfect answers. Our reading lives are meant to crack us open and deepen our own capacity for virtue.

Tip 23: Get Active

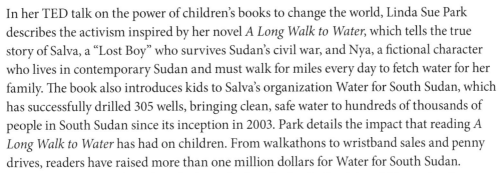

In her TED talk on the power of children's books to change the world, Linda Sue Park describes the activism inspired by her novel *A Long Walk to Water*, which tells the true story of Salva, a "Lost Boy" who survives Sudan's civil war, and Nya, a fictional character who lives in contemporary Sudan and must walk for miles every day to fetch water for her family. The book also introduces kids to Salva's organization Water for South Sudan, which has successfully drilled 305 wells, bringing clean, safe water to hundreds of thousands of people in South Sudan since its inception in 2003. Park details the impact that reading *A Long Walk to Water* has had on children. From walkathons to wristband sales and penny drives, readers have raised more than one million dollars for Water for South Sudan.

While book reading doesn't always lead to this kind of activism, kids need a place to start, to feel they can make a difference in the face of conflict, suffering, or injustice. Sometimes book reading can inspire kids to simply speak up on the behalf of a friend or advocate for small changes inside their communities. Sometimes the shifts are more internal—a more informed understanding or a desire to inquire more deeply into topics or issues that matter to them.

I work with an organization in San Diego called transcenDANCE (a creative youth organization that builds resilience, confidence, and creativity in teenagers through dance and community engagement) and together with their teaching artists and students, I helped develop and direct a performance for the celebration of John Lewis' graphic novel *March* as part of One Book, One San Diego, an innovative literary initiative to build community through the shared experience of reading. In preparation for this event, the transcenDANCE dancers and I read aloud selections from Jacqueline Woodson's lyrical novel and memoir *Brown Girl Dreaming* (2014), paying particular attention to the way small acts can make a huge difference in people's lives—that, in fact, small acts can be revolutionary. We took a close look at a piece toward the end of the novel titled "A Writer," where Jacqueline's teacher told her, "You're a writer. . . . You're a writer. . . . You're a writer" (311–12), which made a profound difference in her life and her path to becoming a real writer.

After looking closely at "A Writer" and using it as a mentor text, we wrote our own stories about a moment when we made a difference in someone's life or when someone made a difference in ours. Instead of grand gestures or slogans, we thought about small acts of impact and told those stories trying on some of Woodson's craft moves: repetition, real dialogue, specific action words like "*bend* into desks," "fingers *fly*," "hands *freeze*," "voice *shakes*" (311–12), and tiny descriptive details like her "*gray* eyes *bright* behind *thin wire* frames" (311). Each student wrote his or her own story and I helped create a script using their original writing, sections of which served as interludes to every dance piece. They wrote about showing up for their friends, their siblings, themselves. "I will never forget that this boy stood up for me," wrote one. "I tell my sister all the time how beautiful and smart she is. I tell her nothing compares to her beautiful chocolate skin," wrote another.

The stories students wrote and shared publicly about their lives were acts of creativity and courage, which is no small feat. In the words of actress Amandla Stenberg, "oftentimes your authenticity is your activism and being as true to yourself as possible is the first step toward revolution" (Lawrence 2016). We can use our read-alouds as springboards for truth telling in our classrooms. By wrapping our collective minds around an issue and looking closely at a particular part of the book as a mentor text or source of inspiration, we can create pieces of writing that give students a platform, a chance to connect their struggles and journeys with the ones they see in books, and perhaps even an opportunity to perform or express those stories in a public way. This is artful activism, all made possible by gathering around a story and reading aloud together.

Tip 24: Share the Power and the Journey

Cornelius Minor reminds us that social justice isn't just in our content. "It's not just that I show up to school and I talk about Civil Rights and I talk about equity. . . . Social justice actually lives in my everyday methodology. How I treat students. How I speak to students.

How I create opportunities for students to be themselves. How I create flexible curriculum for kids to move in and out of depending on their abilities. All of that is justice" (Minor and Richard 2018).

All of our interactions with kids can create a foundation for justice in our schools—or not. Two key ways an interactive read-aloud supports a pedagogy of social justice is that it (1) levels the playing field and (2) gives students a chance to talk about ideas, make meaning, and learn from each other without strict teacher controls. We are sharing the experience with them, allowing their ideas and observations to guide our conversations and our meaning making. We read the book and invite them to do the work. While sometimes that means we are welcoming them to observe our expert reader's mind at work, more of the time we are encouraging them to use their own. As Minor also says, "equity happens in micro-interactions." It can be as simple and as powerful as "taking the time to listen to a kid."

Listening is critical. It makes sense that listening continues to come up throughout this book. The whole enterprise of reading aloud rests on the notion of listening well—to the book, the author, and each member of the class. But the split between our thinking aloud and kids' thinking aloud and conversation should not be fifty-fifty; their conversations and meaning making should outweigh our own.

As we read books that deal with big issues, we must remember that we do not have to have all the answers or all the wisdom. In fact, it's important to make our own learning journey transparent. I am especially aware of this as a white educator. I know how important it is to read books that deal with critical issues around our racialized society and the history of racism in our country, and sometimes that means I make room for complicated conversations where my perspective is limited. I talk openly with students about the voices I am learning from and the ways in which I am seeking to grow my understanding. Building trust with students sometimes starts with being vulnerable and real. One of Zaretta Hammond's tips for building trust across differences is to "share some of your life experiences so they see you as human, not just the authority figure. In return, listen to their stories" (2015). This means it's OK to admit you need to think something over. Hammond also writes,

Don't think you can't talk about black history because you're a white educator. . . . You do not need to be a person of color to talk about race. But you do need to be comfortable in your own skin, build your knowledge about the topic and be in alliance with educators of color for support and feedback. (2013b)

At one of the schools in which I work, we launched a faculty book club and met four times across the year to discuss contemporary children's literature. One of the books we read was *Wishtree* (Applegate 2017), which is told from the perspective a very old northern red oak tree, Red, who witnessed centuries of change inside her community and inside the yards of the two houses she shades. A range of people of varying ethnicities lived in the houses over the years. "Over the years," Red narrates, "many called those houses home. Babies and teenagers, grandparents and great-grandparents. They spoke Chinese and Spanish, Yoruba and English and French Creole. They ate tamales and pani puri, dim sum and fufu and grilled cheese sandwiches." When a ten-year-old girl named Samar and her family moved into the blue house, however, "something changed. The air was uneasy" (55). Samar and her family "were from a distant country. Their ways were unfamiliar. Their words held new music" (55). Some folks in the community did not embrace Samar's family, and one day a "car passed by, filled with angry men yelling angry things like 'Muslims, get out!'" (55).

In our conversation about the book, some of the teachers discussed how uncomfortable they might feel if they were reading *Wishtree* aloud and came upon that part in the story, which is understandable. It feels awful to read aloud hateful words, even in the context of an unfolding story, and how exactly does one do that, or should we? Of course racial slurs or epithets should *never* be read aloud in our K–8 classrooms, even in context. But, in the case of a book like *Wishtree*, I believe we have to let the story do its work. When I come upon places in books that are unsettling, or loaded, my voice tends to gets a little quieter. I try my best to read those parts as straightforwardly as I can, without exaggerating. Most importantly, I read without rushing, which can often happen because we are anxious and want to speed through the discomfort. And then I usually take a breath, a true pause, and invite the students to talk about what they are wondering or feeling. Then I get out of the way again and let them talk and wonder, think and feel, without micromanaging their responses. I let them dwell in the ambiguity without worrying about whether or not we will find our way to closure.

In a sense, I think of myself as the vessel in these moments, not the interpreter. Hopefully all my modeling has made it possible for kids to notice and question together in rich, substantive ways. For sure, these can be complicated, even messy, conversations. But the truth is the kids are already having them! And they need us to show up. Kids need the support and presence of loving adults inside these conversations, even if we can't provide all the answers. We have to be willing to make space in our classrooms for conversations about all kinds of social issues, which is altogether different from indoctrination or advocating along political lines. Using a read-aloud book as a container for such conversations gives them a meaningful context, and in some ways a less intimidating one—talking about big issues that characters are going through or that authors write about feels easier than talking about those same issues as they apply to ourselves. And as Jewell Parker Rhodes (2018) reminded us, it's important to remember that the book is your *partner* in these conversations; we can and should lean on the work the author has already done for us (see Chapter 3 for more on this).

However, we don't want the read-aloud to cause trauma. We have to be responsive to the children in front of us, knowing who they are and choosing wisely. But we also don't want to pretend things don't exist, which sends a different message: that some things are so shameful—or (equally problematic) *insignificant*—that we don't ever speak of them or deal with them up close. As I've said before, a book can be a lifeline, a refuge, a profound reminder to a child that he or she is not alone. And a book can also channel kids toward action and change—sometimes bold and public, other times quiet and internal. But we must remember that more than anything, literacy is about power and agency. An important piece of the artful read-aloud is the space it creates for kids to respond authentically in the community of their peers, which helps kids understand that we read not only to learn and imagine but also to become more courageous, empathic, well-informed, and open-hearted people.

11

Principle Nine

Move Around

Giving kids a chance to live inside the book

Movement anchors thought.

—NEUROPHYSIOLOGIST CARLA HANNAFORD

In my work with the Creative Youth Development organization transcenDANCE, I am often watching rehearsals and witnessing students share their stories, and their inner lives, through movement. I always find it fascinating how students' *voices* emerge during a rehearsal, even though I'm not hearing them speak at all. I asked Cat Corral, founder and artistic director of transcenDANCE, how she makes sense of this. "Sometimes," she wrote to me in an email, "words do not get to the root of what we are feeling or want to say. Sometimes, asking students to respond with movement allows us a glimpse of their spirits that words could not express. Children can breathe life into a memory, a vision, a hope, a color of the day, when we ask them to embody it, move it, dance it, hold a physical shape with it" (September 25, 2018).

We must find ways to help children express what they are thinking, feeling, and want to say. We can give children opportunities to respond to text with their bodies, sharing their ideas through movement. We can also give kids a truly theatrical experience through the read-aloud. It can be a time for kids to move around, make noise, embody the characters and words, and connect deeply with a text through gesture, voice, and physical expression.

In their book *A Reason to Read*, which documents the work of their visionary ArtsLiteracy Project, Eileen Landay and Kurt Wootton write, "A growing body of literature suggests that physical activity plays a significant part in developing cognitive capacity. Challenging the age-old dichotomy between mind and body, neuroscientists, linguists, and philosophers now accept that mimetic activities—movement and gesture—function as fundamental aspects of human intelligence and that moving and thinking are not, as Descartes proposed, separate phenomenon [*sic*]" (2012, 69).

Put more simply, movement really does anchor thought.

Movement is an essential part of the artistic process. Certainly that's true for dancers, but actors, singers, visual artists, even writers root their creative process physically, inside their bodies. I've long been fascinated by acclaimed novelist Lauren Groff's writing process. She writes all of her first drafts by hand on legal pads, which she says helps her "get a sense of the landscape" and discover the cracks in the foundation of her stories (2016a). In a 2016 interview with Charlie Rose, Groff added, "I start building a 3D printer . . . of almost a city of stories, then I can walk through the city, and choose which way to go through. . . . You're building a world." In order to get started on *Fates and Furies*, a novel about marriage told in two distinctly different voices, Groff hung up two pieces of butcher paper on the wall in her Florida studio and would write a scene from the wife's perspective, then find herself "running across the room and writing from the husband's greener point of view" (2016b). The fact that Groff writes by hand and literally runs between perspectives speaks to this idea that our brains and our bodies work in tandem to create or imagine something new or beautiful. Embodiment is the work of artists and learners of all stripes, ages, and abilities.

Tip 25: Invite Kids to Make Movements and Sounds

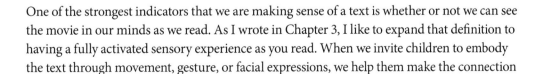

One of the strongest indicators that we are making sense of a text is whether or not we can see the movie in our minds as we read. As I wrote in Chapter 3, I like to expand that definition to having a fully activated sensory experience as you read. When we invite children to embody the text through movement, gesture, or facial expressions, we help them make the connection between reading and the vibrant world we inhabit in our minds. Pretty much every piece of children's literature, whether it's fiction or nonfiction, has places that would make wonderful stopping points to teach or reinforce a word's meaning through gesture or movement, to imagine a character's facial expression and try it out, or to build a mental model of a place, a scene, or a concept with external movement. There is great value in finding such places, not only because kids enjoy movement but also because it is deeply instructional.

K–2 Fiction

When I work with younger children, I almost always invite them to gesture, move around, and make expressions with me as I read, especially because so many vocabulary words are new, they are just starting to learn about character development, and they are typically more than willing to move around.

For example, *Stellaluna* (Cannon 1993) is a classic picture book with very sophisticated vocabulary. Whenever I read it to children, I often pause and invite them to physicalize a word with an accompanying gesture.

> "The story says Stellaluna's wings were *limp* and *useless* as wet paper. Let's all pretend we have *limp* and *useless* wings that feel like wet paper."

> "Let's *clutch* the branch just like Stellaluna does, and some of us might even *tremble* a little bit, just like she does because she is so cold and afraid."

Video 11
First Graders
Move Around
to *Stellaluna*

See p. ix on how to access this video clip and others found in the book.

You'll notice the deep engagement with the story and the words as I invite children to embody the different words, but take a look at Video 11, where we not only embody the word *croon* but sing a little song to our baby Stellaluna bats in a first-grade classroom.

K–2 Nonfiction

Physicalizing or embodying new concepts and vocabulary in nonfiction texts is particularly important and helps children learn new information or ideas. There are countless books about animals that make perfect read-alouds and opportunities to learn new vocabulary. As I read these books, I always invite children to move their bodies to capture the way different animals move, get food, and live in the world.

For example, for *Are You a Snail?* (Allen 2003), I invite children to act out lines such as this one: "You have two horns and eyes on stalks. You can pull your eyes right down inside the stalks and into your head if you need to." I might say, "Let's all imagine those two stalks on our heads with eyes at the end of them! Let's pull those eyes right down inside the stalks and into our heads."

After reading, "You have a shell with a beautiful pattern on it. You have no legs and only one foot, but it is a strong foot. The slime on your strong foot helps you slide along" (10), I might say, "Let's all imagine we have a beautiful pattern on our shells and let's pretend our two fingers are the strong foot of a snail that helps us slide along, leaving behind a trail of slime!" Embodying the technical language or key words (*horns, stalks, pattern, slime*) strengthens children's familiarity with and understanding of them.

Tip 26: Dramatize a Scene, a Picture, or Even a Book

We often ask children to turn and talk after listening to a key moment inside a read-aloud, but some moments or scenes are beautifully suited to being quickly acted out. Reenacting a scene helps them revisit and hold onto what happened and it helps them keep track of the important moments, all of which strengthens their ability to retell or synthesize the story. Reenactment also gives them another way of looking closely at a part to consider its significance and the hidden layers of meaning, both as actors and audience members. Any scene between two characters that is significant or reveals something about their relationship could be a moment to dramatize.

Five Dramatization Structures

1. Reenact a scene.
2. Create a snapshot.
3. Imagine the dialogue or inner monologue.
4. Repeat or reread the dialogue.
5. Stage a picture-book theatre performance.

Reenact a Scene

In the beginning of *Because of Winn-Dixie* (DiCamillo 2000), Opal approaches her father, the "preacher," to ask if she can keep the dog she brought home from the Winn-Dixie grocery store. After I read this scene (which starts with Opal entering the trailer, saying, "Daddy?" and ends with her saying, "But this dog needs me. Look . . . Winn-Dixie!" [17]), I pause and invite children to re-create the moment between the two characters: "That little scene seemed to reveal a lot about those characters and their relationship. Let's see if we can re-create that scene right here on the rug after listening to it again. As I read, listen for what each character says, and imagine how they might look or move while they say it."

I reread the scene and then say, "Partner A, you'll be Opal. Partner B, you'll be the preacher. Turn and act it out using the words from the book." Afterward, I usually choose one partnership to perform for the whole group. This is a great opportunity to let kids who are dramatically or kinesthetically inclined to shine.

Then we discuss. I say, "After watching this little scene again, what are some of the things you noticed? What are you thinking about Opal and her dad? What new ideas might you have about their relationship?"

Re-creating this scene allows children to take a deeper look at the lack of connection between the characters right from the start of the novel. It also helps them understand some of the threads inside the book—and the changing relationship between Opal and her dad is one of the biggest threads inside *Because of Winn-Dixie*.

Create a Snapshot

You could also re-create a moment in freeze-frame fashion, or what I call snapshots. Usually I do this by splitting the class in half, with one half enacting the freeze-frame and the other half watching. Then they switch.

I set it up like this: "Partner As on this side, you're going to show us your snapshot of Opal entering the trailer. Partner Bs on this same side, you'll be the preacher looking at his papers. Get into your characters and freeze!"

I often ask the children to name their thoughts or feelings in character:

"Opal, what are you thinking and feeling here?"

[*To a different child*] "What else are you thinking or feeling here, Opal?"

[*To a third child*] "What do you wish your father would do or say here?"

"What are you thinking about here, Preacher? What's on your mind right now?"

After allowing children to both create and watch a snapshot, I say, "After observing this moment, what are some of the things you noticed? What are you thinking about Opal and her dad? What new ideas might you have about their relationship?"

Neither reenactments nor snapshots require much advanced planning, nor are they meant to go on and on. They provide easy opportunities to look again at an important moment in the book and see more inside of it. No matter the fiction book, you can use similar language to invite kids to re-create a moment in order to take a closer look at the motivations, desires, and struggles of individual characters and the important relationships inside books.

Imagine the Dialogue or Inner Monologue

Picture Books

You could practically take any picture book, find a page with characters speaking or doing something, and invite children to imagine what a character or two might say, what *else* they might say, and what they might feel. Children can easily turn and talk to one another in role, but they can also jot their ideas down as the character on a sticky note, which is a terrific data point and quick, informal assessment of their thinking. I use this strategy frequently with picture books because it helps children develop a much deeper understanding of the internal lives of characters.

There is a heartbreaking moment in *Those Shoes* (Boelts 2009) when the main character, Jeremy, returns to his classroom in his new shoes, given to him by the guidance counselor after his shoes broke apart. The illustration shows Jeremy standing in the doorway and the children laughing at him, all except for one, Antonio. I invite children to take a closer look at Antonio. "What do you think he might be thinking or feeling here?" I ask. "What do you think he might wish he could say? Pretend you are Antonio and turn and tell your partner what's on your mind." Inevitably, children consider Antonio's point of view, his compassion for Jeremy, and even his worry that kids might laugh at his own beat-up shoes. This teaches kids that they can use their imaginations to inhabit a text, a scene, or a picture with depth, that they should consider multiple perspectives, and that there is more to a story than just the narrator's point of view.

Children usually love this kind of dramatic role-playing, but it is more than just engaging for them. For one, it encourages younger children (who are likely still reading books with a lot of picture support) to practice using their imaginations to see beyond the two-dimensional page. This work helps them rev up their minds, get a fuller movie rolling, and remember that the pictures and sounds we see in our reading brains are not stagnant, but moving and ongoing.

But don't reserve this strategy just for younger children. It also helps older children slow down, think inferentially, and consider multiple perspectives—all of which can transfer to their independent reading lives.

Novels

Taking a moment to consider what a character wished she could say or what a character *might* be feeling or thinking is one of my favorite ways to set up a turn-and-talk between partners during read-aloud. For one, it breaks up the routine of turning and talking and instead offers a chance to turn and imagine, or act something out. It also pushes kids to think more inferentially. It is critical that we use this strategy mindfully and respectfully. Delving into the inner life of a character to teach empathy or build a stronger sense of a character's motivations, feelings, or experience is one thing. However, asking kids to take on someone else's culture, identity, or assumed way of speaking is something else entirely. We must always be sensitive to the dynamics and identities within our classrooms before introducing any of these dramatic structures.

There is a moment between Amal and her father in the beginning of *Amal Unbound* (Saeed 2018) where she brings up the possibility of going back to school after staying at home to help care for her mother and little sisters. After reading through this scene with a group of fifth graders, I said, "Let's all step into the role of Amal. What might Amal wish she could say to her father in this moment? What do you think she might be thinking in this moment? Turn and talk." In Video 12, I invite children to imagine what Stella the elephant *might* have whispered in little Rudy's ear when she first arrives on the scene in *One and Only Ivan*.

Once students have a chance to turn and imagine the inner monologue of a character, I sometimes give them a chance to voice their lines. As I encourage different children to share in role, and to add on, I often address them as the character they are inhabiting to reinforce the idea that all of us are playing the role—all of these contributions create a collective, whole-class monologue. (See Figures 11.1 and 11.2, next page.)

Video 12
What *Might* the Character Have Said?

See p. ix on how to access this video clip and others found in the book.

"What are you thinking or feeling right now, Amal?"

"What do you wish you could do or say?"

"What else might Stella say in this moment?"

"Let's add on. Who else can add to this interior monologue?"

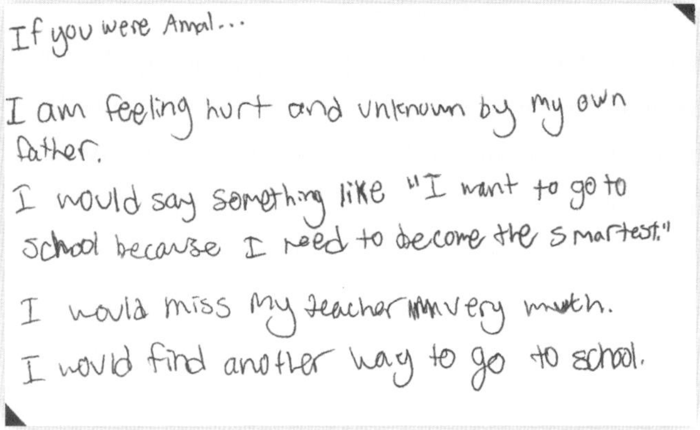

> If you were Amal...
>
> I am feeling hurt and unknown by my own father.
> I would say something like "I want to go to school because I need to become the smartest."
> I would miss my teacher very much.
> I would find another way to go to school.

Figure 11.1 Student Work for *Amal Unbound*

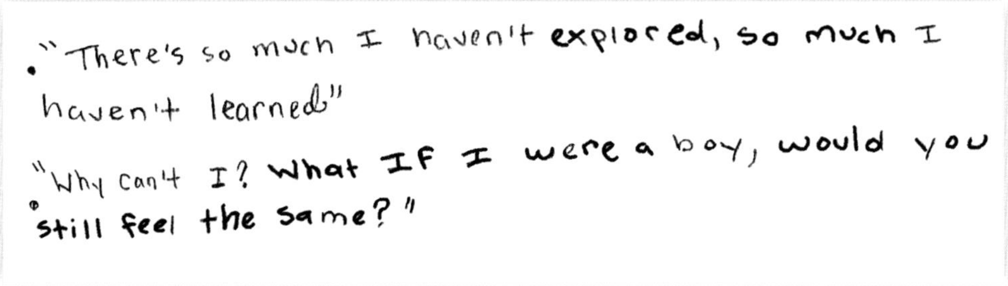

> ."There's so much I haven't explored, so much I haven't learned."
>
> "Why can't I? What IF I were a boy, would you still feel the same?"

Figure 11.2 Student Work for *Amal Unbound*

Repeat or Reread the Dialogue

Repeating the dialogue is a wonderfully engaging strategy, particularly for younger children, that gives them license to take on voices and embody characters. Sometimes characters say things that surprise you, make you laugh, or feel so unique to their personalities that they bear repeating in order to appreciate or understand the characters better. It's simple: when you come across a line or two of dialogue that feels juicy or revealing, invite kids to say it again with you! The way characters speak—or the way we hear them speak in our mind—helps us construct a deeper sense of who they are, how they act, and why they do what they do.

For example, there are some great lines to act out in *Not Norman* (Bennet 2008):

"Look! Norman's singing," I say.
"Pay attention!" snaps Maestro. "And try to play the proper notes."

I love the maestro in this story. We repeat his irritated lines of dialogue, imagine his body language, and then, of course, discuss what the word *maestro* means.

The proper exchange between Mr. Tiger and Mr. Deer in *Mr. Tiger Goes Wild* (Brown 2013) is too good to pass up. We always repeat their lines back and forth in a way that demonstrates what the words *proper* and *formal* mean:

Good day, Mr. Tiger.
Good day, Mr. Deer.
Lovely weather we are having.
I suppose.
Indeed.

It is also possible to create a mini shared reading experience in the middle of the read-aloud by putting the book under the doc cam and just focusing on a snippet of dialogue. Kids can read along or simply join in with you, in addition to discussing the vocabulary words that go along with the dialogue. This can work just as easily when you are reading novels with older children as with picture books, especially if there is a particularly important or meaningful bit of dialogue in the middle of a novel, or if you are practicing skills such as fluency, character analysis, and envisioning. In order to create a mini shared reading experience with older kids, I sometimes split the class up into different roles and read the selection again as the different characters. Other times, I invite individual kids to read the scene out loud, looking at the text under the doc cam. See Videos 13 and 14 for students acting out excerpts from *Stellaluna* (Cannon 1993) and *The One and Only Ivan* (Applegate 2012).

Video 13
Shared Reading: *Stellaluna*

Video 14
Shared Dramatic Reading: *The One and Only Ivan*

See p. ix on how to access these video clips and others found in the book.

Stage a Picture-Book Theatre Performance

Even if you don't have the desire or bandwidth to turn a story into a play, it's easier than you might think to create moments of theatre in your room right there on the fly! In many ways it's an extension of repeating the dialogue, with perhaps a tad more practice and perhaps a few bits of theatrical magic or props thrown in as well. Some of my favorite books to do this with are *Extra Yarn* (Barnett 2012), *Owl Babies* (Waddell 2002), *Last Stop on Market Street* (de la Peña 2015), and *Mr. Tiger Goes Wild* (Brown 2013).

Ten Easy Picture-Book Theatre Steps

1. *Decide how you will sit.* If we are bringing the text to life just for ourselves, we usually sit in a circle and the children act out their parts in the middle. If we are performing for another class or a few invited guests, the children usually sit next to me and I sit on a chair, holding the book.

2. *Choose who will be the different characters.* For *Extra Yarn*, the characters would be Annabelle, the different townspeople, Nate, Mr. Crabtree, Mr. Norman, and the archduke. Children who don't want a specific part can always participate in the whole-group parts or nonspeaking parts. If the book you choose doesn't have that many characters, kids can take turns, or several kids can play the same role at the same time, either in small groups or in partnerships. Or the whole class can embody the roles together, acting out each character and repeating the dialogue as you read. (See Figure 11.3.)

Figure 11.3

3. *Find lines in the book that make sense for the whole class to say along with you.* This gives even more kids a chance to participate—especially those who are reluctant to say or do anything on their own. Often these lines are ones that relate to the big idea in the book or are the final lines of the story. (See Video 15.)

4. *When a character is introduced in the story, have the children playing that role stand in preparation to perform.* As you read, children can act out their part. In *Extra Yarn*, Annabelle would pretend to find a box with yarn inside and begin to knit after you read the opening lines. As you continue, children can stand up when they hear their part and either stay put or start physicalizing the action. (See Figure 11.4.)

5. *Read the full line of dialogue and allow children to repeat the line in character.* Usually I go line by line so kids don't need to worry about remembering and can focus on embodying the character. You could of course read more than one line of dialogue at at time before children say them aloud themselves. For whole-group lines, you can either say them first, or if kids have them down, they might just say them along with you. (See Video 16.)

Video 15
Children
Repeat Words

Video 16
Children
Repeat Lines
of Dialogue

See p. ix on how to access these video clips and others found in the book.

Figure 11.4

Video 17
The Whole Class Participates in Read-Aloud

See p. ix on how to access this video clip and others found in the book.

6. *Find places where the* whole *class can participate, say a line, make sound, or move around.* In *Extra Yarn*, the whole class can play the whispering and distracted schoolchildren during the school scene. I've also had all the kids play the animals that Annabelle makes sweaters for by barking and meowing after the lines, "She made sweaters for all the dogs [*"Bark!"*] and all the cats [*"Meow!"*] and for other animals too [*various animal sounds and actions*]" (16). (See Figure 11.5.) (See Video 17.)

7. *Decide upon and practice a bit of simple blocking if necessary or desired.* Where might a character move or end up as you are reading? In *Extra Yarn*, the child playing the archduke goes to a specific spot that marks his castle far away. He also throws the empty box back into the sea in slow motion and then makes his furious way back to his spot and sits back down. You don't need a large stage to make this possible; allowing children to act out or physicalize the movements even in a very limited space works just fine.

8. *When useful (or fun!), embody the inanimate objects inside the text.* In *Extra Yarn*, the children become the sea, across which the empty box is thrown, by waving their arms. Sometimes I even invite them to embody the archduke's

Figure 11.5

mustache! They put their hands on their own imaginary mustaches and show how it "quivered, shivered, and trembled" (Barnett 2012, 29).

9. *Sprinkle in some theatre magic (without spending any money)!* Are there any places to use a cool prop or set piece? It's amazing what you can make with the tools and supplies in your own classroom. Students who have performed *Extra Yarn* with me have used a dry-erase marker box as Annabelle's box of yarn and colorful dry-erase markers to symbolize the sweaters and scarves she knits. We've also taken approximately five minutes to draw a black-and-white city on a whiteboard. In the middle of the story, when "things began to change in that little town" (19) all the children have gotten up and added color to the whiteboard picture with their dry-erase markers to represent the way in which Annabelle's knitting (and imagination!) trans-formed the town. (See Figure 11.6.)

10. *Rehearse once or twice and go for it!* No need to belabor! Invite another class to watch and then have a discussion or reflection on the book. This kind of informal theatrical experience gives all the children participating (as actors and audience members) a shared experience around a text to discuss and truly understand, which serves as a touch-stone for what really comprehending a text feels like.

Figure 11.6

Whenever I work with teachers or graduate students to create read-aloud theatre, I focus on the importance of *play* and *creativity*! Instead of aiming for something that is a perfectly polished production, we try to bring the story to life by incorporating these five principles:

1. *Transformation.* How can we transform the space we are in? How can we transform the objects we have around us? How can we create a transformative experience for the participants and the audience?

2. *Connection.* How can we use this experience with literature to feel more connected to one another? How

can we create an experience that connects children to the words, the story, and the love of reading?

3. *Comprehension.* How does this experience help children understand the text more deeply? What can I ask them to notice or think about during and afterward that might strengthen their comprehension?

4. *Embodiment.* Where can I include moments for children to embody the text, to physicalize the actions, and to move around and step inside the story?

5. *Joy.* How can this be a joyful, engaging experience for kids, the audience, and me?

Tip 27: Create Readers Theatre Using Stand-Out Scenes

With the boon of spectacular children's literature being written these days, chapter books can function as gorgeous scripts! Creating readers theatre *with* children using young adult novels instead of prefabricated readers theatre books (which are usually flat and not very well written) helps them strengthen a whole host of reading skills through purposeful, engaging work together. Readers theatre is a wonderful strategy for kids of all ages, but I often hand over the creative process to older kids so they can make all the artistic and literary choices in small groups, which gives them opportunities to direct themselves, incorporate movement, and closely read passages from their books again.

When you finish reading a novel aloud, it's the perfect opportunity to celebrate the book by turning several beloved or significant scenes into readers theatre. Before asking students to try this, I model by putting the book under the doc cam and showing how to pencil in the different parts. As a class we practice a scene as a shared reading exercise and with different kids or groups speaking the different parts. I also show them that sometimes it's better to cross out "he said" and "she said" when characters are speaking to keep the flow of dialogue. And when characters do things as they speak, sometimes it makes more sense to actually embody that action instead of reading it aloud.

Once children get the hang of creating readers theatre with the books we read aloud, they can apply it with the books they read independently, especially when they are in book clubs. As clubs make their way through a book, they can reread a scene as readers theatre as part of their discussion time in order to get conversation started, think again about an important part, or notice more about a particular moment or exchange. At the end of a book, clubs can reflect back over the book and determine which scenes were pivotal moments, which scenes spoke to the big themes, or which scenes felt particularly memorable and perform them as a club or for other classmates. At the end of the year, clubs might decide to perform a selection of readers theatre scenes to celebrate their favorite books across the year. These informal performances can be just within your classroom, or you can use them to promote books for younger classes or to share the students' reading lives with an audience of family members.

Readers theatre is a highly engaging way for students to improve and practice their reading fluency, which is strongly linked to their reading comprehension. Professor Tim Rasinski (2012), a leading expert in the role and importance of fluency, writes about the value of reading wide and deep. It's essential for children to read many texts, from a variety of genres (wide), and also to read one text repeatedly (deep) in order to read with automaticity and expression, both of which lead to deep comprehension. Students need practice hearing their own strong, expressive voice when they read a passage repeatedly because it helps them to hear a strong, expressive voice when they read independently and silently. "Through repeated reading," Rasinski writes, "readers become more adept and efficient at employing prosodic features into new passages not previously read" (519). Not only do kids enjoy the process of choosing and rehearsing their readers theatre scenes, which ultimately helps them make more meaning out of that particular text and remember it with clarity, but it has an effect on their future reading as well! I love a win-win.

Reading with prosody is not to be underestimated. According to Rasinski, "readers at the third-, fourth-, fifth-, and eighth-grade levels who read orally with good prosody also tend to be good comprehenders when reading silently. Conversely . . . studies have found that readers who read with poor prosody (in a monotone and word-by-word manner) also have poor comprehension when reading silently" (519). Rasinski also writes that "a growing number of studies are demonstrating that fluency is a major concern for students in grades 4 and 5, in middle school, and in high school" (521). If you want to give students purposeful and enjoyable opportunities for repeated reading, creating readers theatre scripts out of the books you read aloud or the books students read on their own is an easy and valuable strategy, especially for students in upper elementary and middle school.

Directions for Creating Readers Theatre in Small Groups or Book Clubs

Once kids have the idea for how readers theatre goes after practicing as a whole class, I give them these guidelines for creating readers theatre with their book clubs.

1. Discuss with your group: What scene or scenes will you put on its feet? What scenes will you choose to pair together? What do these choices reveal about the book, the character(s), and the themes in this book?

2. Decide which roles everyone will play. How many narrators will there be? Decide which parts each narrator says. Cut out any unnecessary "he saids" and "she saids" in order to create a more natural flow of dialogue. See Figure 11.7.

3. Decide what lines the whole group will say together. There should be at least one.

4. Find places to add movement or gesture in order to help your audience envision the action of this scene.

5. Do your best to have fun! Sprinkle in some unexpected movements, props, or theatre magic.

6. Discuss what new ideas, thoughts, or questions you have after choosing, practicing, and performing the scene together.

Figure 11.7 Annotated Readers Theatre Text

In addition to improving fluency, readers theatre also provides a purposeful context in which to deepen a whole host of comprehension skills:

Determining importance. Which part is important enough to put on its feet? Which line seems important enough to say all together? Which line seems to convey the main idea of this passage? What should we do with that line or how should we say it?

Envisioning and inferring. How would a character speak this line or physicalize this action?

Synthesizing. How have the characters changed throughout the book? How has the story changed?

Interpreting. What are the big themes and ideas in this book? What scenes reveal the big ideas in this book?

Some of my favorite books to use as readers theatre with younger children are the Elephant and Piggie series, by Mo Willems; they have no narration and are some of the funniest scripts you'll ever read! If you have one copy, two children can gather together and decide who will read Piggie and who will read Gerald, which is easy because their speech bubbles are different colors. Often there are three characters in these books, so you could also create some groups of three.

The Mercy Watson books, by Kate DiCamillo, are equally funny and also easy to turn into scripts. They would make perfect practice for older children who need support with their fluency or who are reading below grade level, especially if they perform them for younger children. Each chapter usually consists of two to three characters and a narrator or two, so children can read them like scripts in small groups. Children playing the narrator can read the exposition. This could just as easily work with other early series books featuring two to three main characters, such as Arnold Lobel's Frog and Toad or Cynthia Rylant's Mr. Putter and Tabby books.

As you look through the books in your libraries or peruse new books, consider ways you might bring them to life. When I read *Wishtree* by Katherine Applegate, I immediately thought—This is a play! Right away I could imagine lots of kids playing the role of Red the tree, saying lines individually and some all together. Each child playing Red could also hold a branch and everyone else could play the townspeople! The same thing happened with *Extra Yarn*—this would make a beautiful piece of theatre! Read your books with fresh eyes: How might you get kids up and out of their chairs and invite them to step into the world of the book through embodiment? Not only will your books come alive, but your kids and your classroom will too!

12

Principle Ten

Choose Wisely

Being intentional about your choices

**Each decision we make, each action we take,
is born out of an intention.**

—SHARON SALZBERG

For most of my life, I have been on both sides of theatrical experiences. Sometimes I've been one of the creators or performers, and other times I've been an audience member watching the work unfold. Something that always intrigues me is the journey that any piece undergoes: from a tiny idea to a fully realized performance or piece of art. I love hearing artists talk about what started them off on their creative journey or process. Did you know that E. B. White noticed a spider web in his barn in Maine, cut down the egg sac, put it in a candy box, brought it back to New York City, and watched with delight as hundreds of spiderlings escaped through the air holes of the candy box and spun webs all around his apartment (Corrigan 2011)? Or that Lin-Manuel Miranda picked up Ron Chernow's biography of Hamilton at an airport bookstore, read it on vacation, and got the idea for a hip-hop musical about the founding fathers as a result (Mead 2015)?

Works of art don't appear out of thin air, and it's fascinating to hear about how ideas come to be. We can imagine the hours of writing at the desk or rehearsing at the piano. We can imagine, too, the hours any painter or sculptor spends working and reworking his colors or clay. What we often never know is what got cut along the way, what hard choices an artist had to make on her creative journey. Any piece of art is made up of a million tiny choices and sometimes difficult, even painful ones. I've worked on a lot of new musicals and I've seen how agonizing it was for the writers to let go of songs that were gorgeous and beloved but just didn't move the story along or serve the piece as a whole. In a *New York Times* profile about Jerome Robbins, one of the greatest American choreographers, directors, and dancers, the author quotes Frederick Ashton, a fellow dance legend from Britain, as saying, "It's not what you put into a ballet; it's what you leave out" (Macaulay 2018). The author continues by pointing out

> *few choreographers were more audacious than Robbins in these good deeds of omission. You can pull off such master strokes effectively only if what you're doing has imagination and vision. (Macaulay 2018)*

If we are to pull off master strokes in our read-alouds, we have to have imagination and vision. We have to make choices about what works best and remember that sometimes our omissions are as important as the things we decide to include. As is true with all our teaching moves, we must remember to choose wisely.

Tip 28: Remember It's an Orchestra

If you have noticed that I have contradicted myself throughout this book, you are right.

- Model your powerful thinking aloud, but don't take up too much airtime!
- Don't let turn-and-talks go on too long, but make sure you give thinking enough time!
- Move around, but also create moments of spellbinding silence!
- Be passionate but also intellectual and of course emotionally vulnerable and available too.

As with most things, it's about balance. As much as I believe in the importance of expressing our true love with literature and reading, our read-alouds can't be all passion and love with no substance or rigor. We could love read-aloud up all day and do very little in the way of teaching students about deep noticing or effective analysis. Kids need both. Kids need time to listen and time to talk. It's not either-or. It's both-and. We need to model comprehension strategies by thinking aloud *and* just reading with expression and our whole bodies. We need to pause to clarify *and* sometimes just let the words do their magic.

The read-aloud is like an orchestra: a whole host of comprehension strategies and emotional responses in action. Minilesson and small-group strategy work usually call out one specific instrument. Kids need both. As adult readers, we don't pick up a book and decide that just for today we will focus only on inferring about characters and skip envisioning for the time being. The whole orchestra plays! Whenever we read, we are drawing upon many intellectual, emotional, physical, even spiritual capacities in order to make meaning from the text. The truth is, you could do any number of things at any given time as you read aloud because reading aloud is an integration of *all* the skill work you are teaching at the same time, but you have to make intentional choices about what and when to demonstrate, what comprehension skills to highlight, where to invite kids to talk, and how long both of those things should take. Keep in mind that you can always return to a part of the book on another day if you feel you have missed an opportunity to teach an important skill, or if you feel some children (if not all!) might benefit from a targeted lesson in either reading or writing.

How to Mine One Passage for Multiple Teaching Points

As I read aloud the following scene from *Amal Unbound* (Saeed 2018), I am not going to interrupt the flow. Of course I am hoping, and trusting, that kids are envisioning as I read and that they are experiencing a wide range of emotions. Powerful moments like these can, however, serve as touchstones to be returned to later in other teaching contexts. Once kids have experienced and been moved by the orchestra, *then* you can unpack any number of individual teaching points from a moment that is already familiar. Read the following excerpt, and then see some examples of how I might use it as a touchstone in other teaching lessons or conferences.

> *As I stepped inside, it felt like the past few months had been a terrible nightmare. And now it was over.*
>
> *I was home. . . .*
>
> *Seena peeled a cucumber by the stove. She turned to hush them. That's when she saw me. She gasped. Her knife clattered to the ground.*

"Amal!" she shouted. She rushed toward me and wrapped me in a hug. I had forgotten what it was like to feel someone's embrace.

"Baji's here!" Rabia and Safa shrieked in unison. Their eyes lit up like a string of lights on Eid. They dashed toward me. I picked them both up and hugged them. I didn't know how I would ever let go.

"Amal?"

My mother. She carried my little sister Lubna in her arms. Her hair was loose and damp, grayer than it had been three months earlier. She walked toward me and stroked my hair as if checking to make sure I was real. Then, her expression crumbled. She folded me into her arms. (156–57)

- *Reading minilesson or small group:*
  - *Envisioning.* I want students to pay attention to characters' actions, so I could say, "As I read this, practice making a movie in your mind. Pay careful attention to the specific actions each character takes. Those action words help us create images in our brains that are alive and vivid as we read or listen to the story."
  - *Character development and inference.* If I want to pay attention to characters' reactions, I might say, "As I read, pay attention to the ways the different characters react to Amal's return. What do their reactions show us about how they have changed or how Amal's absence has affected them? Paying attention to these little clues about how characters are described and how they react gives us important information about them."
  - *Fluency.* If I want students to read the lines with expression, trying to make their voices match the emotions of the scene, I could say, "Let's continue reading this scene between Amal and her mother with [student 1] reading the words Amal says out loud, [student 2] reading the words Amal says as the narrator but not out loud, [student 3] reading the role of Amal's mother, and [student 4] reading the role of Rabia. Let's try to make our voices reflect the emotions of each character."
- *Writing workshop.* If I want my writers to think about how to use action words to slow down a moment and help their readers really see it, I might say, "Let's

look again at the way Aisha Saeed slows down this moment. Let's look at all the precise action words that describe exactly what's happening. Look how she describes the moment of Seena seeing her. She doesn't write, 'Seena saw me first.' Instead, she describes all of the tiny actions to help us imagine exactly what happened: 'peeled a cucumber,' 'turned to hush,' 'saw me,' 'gasped,' 'knife clattered,' 'rushed,' 'wrapped.' When you are describing a moment, try to slow down and describe each action, so that your readers can really see it."

It can be tricky to know how much to stop and when and where to call out teaching points versus when to just live inside the moment of the story. Here's the thing: If you actually read aloud every day for at least one solid chunk of precious and protected minutes, you'll develop a rich repertoire of tools and will create opportunities for all different kinds of responses and meaning making because you'll be *doing it every day*. You couldn't possibly invite kids to reenact a moment from a book; add thinking to a Literary Backpack; model your thinking; invite them to turn and talk about their predictions and big ideas; let the words wash over the room by reading without stopping; and also reread a passage of breathtaking beauty all in one day! But, across many days, across an entire year, and across many years in school? Absolutely! When we all commit to reading aloud every day in our classrooms, kids will have opportunities to engage with text in multiple modalities, with deep meaning, and with deep purpose.

Starting a novel always goes a little bit slower than it does once we're inside of it, because then kids have their pictures up and running, and we have spent some time mapping out who is who and how people are related to one another. If I read a novel like *Amal Unbound* every day for fifteen to thirty minutes (which accounts for those days with longer whole-group conversations), I would likely get through it in four to six weeks. When I taught fourth grade, I would usually get through at least two novels before Thanksgiving. I'd choose a shorter novel to read in December and during the weeks leading up to the winter break. Between January and June, I usually read three to four more novels with picture books and other short texts alongside and in between. By the second or third read-aloud, the characters and novels became reference points for the subsequent read-alouds, and the classroom began to fill with new characters and people that felt like members of our community. Students also became more familiar with the routines, structures, and ways of gathering together to think, engage, and interact.

Tips for Middle School Teachers

Middle school teachers are often managing schedules that aren't as flexible as those in younger grades. Middle school teachers who are beginning to incorporate more reading aloud can simply plan to read aloud for about one hour a week, even if that means one day is just five minutes, to continue the momentum and keep the story alive in kids' hearts and imaginations. Shifting the way you spend your time in middle school classrooms can be difficult, but thinking creatively is helpful. The time you spend reading aloud can be flexible and tailored to the demands of your schedule. Here's one way a week's read-aloud time might go:

Monday: Ten minutes to open class, get connected, settle and focus the room, and spark interest and engagement.

Tuesday: Same as Monday.

Wednesday: Five minutes because this is a crazy day. You have a big project or assignment or something that is pressing.

Thursday: Twenty minutes. At the beginning of your read-aloud practice, you might not feel comfortable doing an interactive read-aloud for a full twenty minutes, but you might consider finding one or two days a week where you can have a meatier read-aloud, get through more text, and gain some traction with your thinking, engagement, and conversations.

Friday: Fifteen minutes. This may also be a day where you can have a longer conversation about everything you have read in the week, which means you might read for eight to ten minutes and talk together for the rest.

Kids in middle school don't usually gather on the rug for a read-aloud, but we can still create a feeling of community and connection around the text by positioning ourselves alongside different table groups as we read.

To those who say there is no time for reading aloud because there are other important curricular goals to hit, we must articulate the ways in which those goals are authentically integrated into the interactive read-aloud. If we see reading aloud as central not only to the curriculum but also to the needs of students both as individual readers and as members of a literary community, then we are not finding time for something extra; we are simply choosing to value something that we know has a powerful impact on their reading lives and development. We are choosing to include something in our daily schedule that we know is highly engaging and meaningful for our students. We are letting kids experience the whole orchestra because we know it is one of the most effective and beautiful ways to wrap our hearts, our brains, and our whole communities around text. We are choosing an experience that gives our kids access to thinking, conversation, and meaning making, all of which fuels their independent reading lives. I hope this language helps if you ever find yourself in a situation where you need to defend your choice to read aloud to students every day!

Tip 29: Be Intentional

There are many ways to be intentional about choices we make as we prepare and implement our daily read-alouds. The first, and perhaps most important, is book choice. We must think carefully about what the best text is for this unit, this group, this moment in the school year, or this moment in time.

We must also choose books that reflect a wide variety of voices, genres, authors, and points of view. We must remember the beautiful principle of creating windows and mirrors for our students by filling our classrooms with books that reflect back the experiences, cultures, family structures, losses, dreams, injustices, and joys of our kids, as well as books that help kids imagine and understand the lives, voices, and perspectives of people who are unlike them, who have grown up or live in unfamiliar places or historical times. These windows and mirrors make it possible for kids to see value in themselves and also see beyond themselves. They make it possible for kids to experience and understand that we are connected through story and through our common humanity.

As you are deciding on your read-alouds for the year, you might ask yourself:

- What skills or strategies do I want children to practice in particular? What books would be a good fit for that work?

- What experience do I want to create in the room: One that makes us laugh and bond? One that helps us think about what kind of community we are and want to be? What books would be a good fit for that?

- What other content across the day do I want to support? What book might give kids an entry point into some of the conceptual knowledge or information that will help them along that path?

- How can I include my students' needs, interests, or opinions about what to read aloud next before I get started in a new book?

In a discussion about inclusion, equity, and social justice in school, Cornelius Minor, author of *We Got This*, talks about how essential it is that we bring books into our classrooms that reflect the world of our students, and the world at large, no matter who is in your room. "Even if those kids aren't in the classroom, those books *have* to be in the classroom. Lots of people look around their classrooms and they'll say, 'There are no gay kids here so I don't need books with gay protagonists.' Yes you do. 'There are no black kids here so I don't need books with black protagonists.' Yes you do. 'There are no immigrants here so I don't need books with immigrant protagonists.' Yes you do. Even if you've got a classroom full of white folks—how are we going to have antiracist white people or white people who understand the immigrant experience if we don't expose them to books?" (Minor and Richard 2018).

While I was writing this book, I often read quotes or little passages of text to my mom, a forty-year veteran teacher, and those words rang out for her so profoundly. "Wow," she said after a long pause. "When I think back over my years in the classroom, I'm not sure I was as mindful about this as I should have been." My mom's clarity and honesty was so touching to me, and it's a reminder to all of us that sometimes we need to reflect on the unexamined choices we are making about the books that fill our libraries and that are used as read-alouds. The choices we make about the texts that we bring into our classroom are some of the most powerful ones we can make. With every book you consider for read-aloud, ask yourself:

1. Who or what is the story or book about?
2. Who wrote the book?
3. From whose point of view is this book written?
4. Whom might this book be a mirror for; whom might this book be a window for? How might it be both for lots of different kids?

Making sure to read aloud a balance of books that are written from the point of view of children of color and white children is nonnegotiable. Also nonnegotiable is noticing if a book you've chosen is told from the *point of view* of a child of color but *written* by a white author. Are you are also making sure to choose books written by *authors* of color? If you notice you have read three books in a row that only reflected traditional family structures, what books might make a good choice next? Are you making sure to include books about children of color that reflect the "everyday beauty of being a little human being of color" as well as books that center on civil rights, social justice, and important first achievements? In her op-ed piece "Black Kids Don't Want to Read About Harriet Tubman All the Time," Denene Miller reminds us that children of color "want to read books that engage with their everyday experiences, featuring characters who look like them. Just like any other child" (2018, 10). Furthermore, she writes, "white children, too, deserve—and need—to see black characters that revel in the same human experiences that they do. Real diversity would celebrate the mundane—like a little kid going out after a snowstorm—rather than the exceptional" (10).

You might need to forego a book you love to read one that is less familiar in order to represent a fuller spectrum of human voices, experiences, and points of view. Let me be clear: this is not about checking off boxes of voices you have represented, but about developing a mindfulness, about paying attention to how your choices reflect the spectrum of our shared humanity.

You may have guessed that I absolutely adore anything that Kate DiCamillo writes, but I also love Katharine Applegate, Lauren Wolk, Kimberly Brubaker Bradley, Cynthia Lord, and Lois Lowry. Each one of those authors is phenomenal, and so many of their books would make perfect read-alouds for upper-grade classrooms. But, these authors are all white women. And obviously, I absolutely cannot nor would I ever just read the work of white women aloud. The canon of children's literature is incredibly diverse. If you don't know the organizations We Need Diverse Books and #1000BlackGirlBooks (started by an amazing eleven-year-old named Marley Dias, who was sick of "reading about white boys and dogs"), look them up (Roy 2016).

Once we decide what we might read aloud and begin planning, we face a whole host of other decisions: where to think aloud and what to model, where to invite children into conversation, what moments we might reread, what words or passages we might embody. And *as* we read aloud, we also make choices about how long to let a conversation continue, whose thinking or partnership talk to highlight, and when to linger and when to move on. As I do this work, I think of the words of Frederick Ashton: "It's not what you put into a ballet; it's what you leave out" (Macaulay 2018). Sometimes our best intentions end up cluttering our read-alouds, so we must be as mindful about the moments when we choose to *do* something as we are about the moments when we decide to leave well enough alone. In her book *Teaching Talk*, Kara Pranikoff (2017) offers wise advice about places that often make meaningful stopping points for conversation (a character has a strong emotion; something unexpected is revealed) versus places that don't necessarily merit stopping (new vocabulary is introduced or something confusing comes up).

It can also be helpful to clarify for yourself when you might choose to simply think aloud instead of stopping for conversation. These are times I'm more likely to just think aloud:

- In the beginning of the year, when I am revving up expectations for the thinking work I'll be asking students to try on and learn. I want them to have concrete examples of what to aim for in their jots, turn-and-talks, conference conversations, and silent conversations with themselves.

- When I'm modeling a new strategy or skill that kids need explicit demonstration with, at all levels of text.

- If the text complexity takes a jump from what prior read-alouds demanded, I will demonstrate how my thinking becomes more sophisticated and nuanced.

- When I am modeling strategies and skills students might have practiced in grades or years prior but which I have never modeled, so that it can serve as a mentor text for what I'm hoping they can begin to apply in their independent reading lives across a unit or across the year.

- In the beginning of more complicated books, especially if kids are new to books at levels N and above. I want them to see how my mind makes sense of more complicated texts and opening chapters.

The more you read aloud, the more you begin to develop a felt sense for when to stop, when to come up for air, when to move on, when to rely on your voice and body, when to pause to unpack or think aloud, when to invite kids to talk, and when to let a whole-group conversation emerge. Like anything, your intuition gets stronger with practice. And your choices become more astute.

Tip 30: Respond to Who's in Front of You

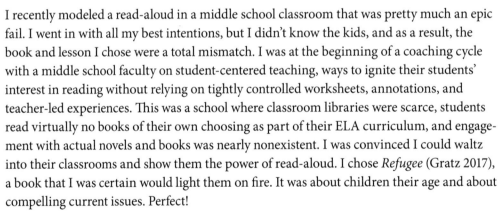

I recently modeled a read-aloud in a middle school classroom that was pretty much an epic fail. I went in with all my best intentions, but I didn't know the kids, and as a result, the book and lesson I chose were a total mismatch. I was at the beginning of a coaching cycle with a middle school faculty on student-centered teaching, ways to ignite their students' interest in reading without relying on tightly controlled worksheets, annotations, and teacher-led experiences. This was a school where classroom libraries were scarce, students read virtually no books of their own choosing as part of their ELA curriculum, and engagement with actual novels and books was nearly nonexistent. I was convinced I could waltz into their classrooms and show them the power of read-aloud. I chose *Refugee* (Gratz 2017), a book that I was certain would light them on fire. It was about children their age and about compelling current issues. Perfect!

Not so much. While *Refugee* is riveting, the beginning chapters are chock-full of facts, dates, and information about the brewing crisis that led to each child's current situation. While the story of each child gets started right away, you have to wade through some complex and technical information first. It didn't grab them; it didn't ignite them; it didn't give them joy. For a first read-aloud with a classroom full of sixth graders whom the teachers described as reluctant readers, I should have chosen a book that would speak to them right away, that didn't have the same text qualities that pushed them away in the first place—unfamiliar facts and information that felt confusing and overwhelming and interrupted their enjoyment of a great story. Or I should have set the stage better by reading aloud and exploring stories about refugees through picture books or the United Nations magazine for kids about the current crisis, all of which would have given them background knowledge and a familiarity with some of the context surrounding each child's story in *Refugee.*

Inspired by my own epic fail, I decided a better choice would have been *The Epic Fail of Arturo Zamora* (Cartaya 2018), a funny, contemporary, bighearted book that sounds like the kids we teach—a book that would have reflected their humor, their struggles, and their friendships. I might have also chosen a book with interesting visuals. In *The First Rule of Punk* (Pérez 2018), the author includes pictures of the main character Malu's zines, which are both artistic and a bit sardonic—perfect for middle school kids. Any one of Kwame Alexander's books, where the story and the language resonate and sparkle immediately, would have also worked beautifully. If I had started my coaching cycle with one of those books, I believe I would have made an entirely different impression. I think I would have shown them books can be world-changing and completely engaging. Alternatively, I could have shown them that books can bring us together in community, can make us happy and laugh, can make us eager to find out what will happen. I think I would have garnered a little bit more buy-in because all of those books are totally compelling rides and not taxing the way that *Refugee* might have felt initially for this particular class of kids. I think I might have set the stage for a book like *Refugee* down the line, because I would have convinced them that books can be worth the effort.

Good teaching is always responsive. It always asks us to pay close attention to what is in front of us and adjust our expectations. I think the best teachers are the ones that share the gift of "animal cunning"—a description that has been given to Mark Rylance, one of the greatest Shakespearean, stage, and screen actors of our generation. Tim Carroll, who has collaborated with Rylance for years and directed him in ten Shakespearean productions, describes Rylance's animal cunning as that which gives him the ability to "smell the room and shape his performance accordingly" (Isherwood 2013, 6). This is precisely what we do when we teach and when we read aloud in particular. If I had planned to read through to the end of the chapter without stopping but then read the room and realized the kids needed a chance to shift their bodies and talk for a minute, I'd give them that break. Or if I had planned a think-aloud or a turn-and-talk but could see the kids were completely enthralled as I was reading, I might continue reading a bit more, maybe to the end of the chapter, before inviting them to discuss or thinking aloud.

Being responsive is actually about putting into practice what we are teaching children to do as readers: to notice, to think and wonder, to reflect and possibly revise or change course along the way. The better we are at noticing and responding, the more aligned our teaching will be with the needs and lives of our kids—and the wiser our decisions will be.

Finale

The magic of theatre—of great theatre, which is what we're aiming for always . . . [is to] have each person just open up a little more than before they walked into the theatre. Their hearts and minds, you know?

—KERRY WASHINGTON, ACTRESS

A great piece of theatre, or any work of art, can affect us, can make us see something in an altogether new way, can open us up and remind us we are not alone. Read-aloud matters so much because it has all the qualities of a great work of art, if we treat it as such. Read-aloud matters because it cuts through the noise. It's simple and accessible to everyone and can light a fire like nothing else. There are so many newfangled distractions in the world these days that seem to threaten our ability to connect, to consider another human being's point of view, to bask in the simple yet transformative glory of listening and talking about a great book together. To read aloud well, we have to be really present, we have to listen and pay close attention, and we have to be willing to learn something new and walk in someone else's shoes.

But mostly, read-aloud matters because it is a way for us to get close to one another. As Brene Brown says, "People are hard to hate close up" (2017, 63). Every day, I read stories in the news that break my heart wide open and shake my faith in our ability to heal the divisions that exist all around us, all throughout the world. Call me crazy, but I think our world leaders could really use a good read-aloud. Imagine them all, in their suits and practical heels, mouths slightly ajar as they are transported into another time and place, their hearts cracking open and their eyes finding one another as they turn and talk about Louisiana Elefante's despair, Amal's quiet courage, or *Last Stop on Market Street*'s message that perhaps we need to search for beauty in places that we often don't think to look.

One of the best ways to find beauty in places we often don't think to look is to simply listen to one another's stories. In 2012, Pulitzer Prize–winning author Colum McCann founded the organization Narrative 4 in an effort to harness the power of story exchange to help young people improve their own lives, their communities, and the world. In the story exchange, individuals are randomly paired up, sometimes with opposite worldviews (gun owners and parents who have lost children to gun violence, police officers and teenagers, etc.), and each person shares a defining story from his or her life. After sharing, each person is responsible for taking on their partner's persona and telling his or her story in the first person. "The one true democracy we have is storytelling," McCann says (Bloomgarden-Smoke 2013). "It goes across borders, boundaries, genders, wealth, race—everyone has a story to tell." When we read aloud, we help children understand that everyone has a story and we give them a chance to get up close to people and ideas in books that open them up just a bit more than when they walked in the door.

I wrote earlier about Boston Philharmonic conductor Benjamin Zander (2017), who describes his job as one that "awakens possibility in other people." I saved the rest of the quote for here, the finale:

> *The conductor doesn't make a sound. He depends for his power on his ability to make other people powerful. . . .*
>
> *I realized my job was to awaken possibility in other people. . . . I wanted to know whether I was doing that. And you know how you find out? You look at their eyes. If their eyes are shining, you know you're doing it. If the eyes are not shining, you get to ask a question. . . . Who am I being that my players' eyes are not shining? . . .*
>
> *I have a definition of success. For me, it's very simple. It's not about wealth and fame and power. It's about how many shiny eyes I have around me.*

What we teachers do is hard, and none of us is going to get wealthy, famous, or powerful doing it. But I have a feeling most of us are in it for the shining eyes as well. We are in it because we believe there is something profound about helping to shape the life of a child, about bearing witness to the huge shifts a young person makes inside of a year, about every creative act that a good teacher does throughout the day. The read-aloud is a time of day when shining-eyes moments occur time and time again, when we can take an actual breath and think to ourselves, "Yes, this is why I chose this path, this profession. Yes, this is what really matters: To gather in this way, to let the words of this book alter the air inside this room, to lift us up out of whatever preoccupation or trouble is nibbling away at us. To remind us that there is something greater to attend to and that our reading lives are meant to enrich us and connect us, to stretch us and make us wise."

Reading aloud artfully is an opportunity to create moments in our classrooms that are instructional and intentional, but also *special*. Our read-alouds of course function as models for fluent reading and opportunities for kids to talk and have access to sophisticated text. But they are about so much more than that. Read-alouds help kids experience something that brings them closer to one another and to themselves, and remind them that artistry is always within their reach. By reading artfully, we are modeling how we can approach our texts, but also our lives, with intention and deep curiosity. Our reading lives are an inspiration to our students, of course, but so too are our creative lives and our creative choices. The read-aloud gives us practice living and thinking creatively because it asks us to do what artists do—listen well, notice deeply, make meaning, stay open, dig deep, feel dazzled, move around, and look up. This is the work of real readers, but it is the work of human beings, and all of us can learn not only to read artfully but to live that way too.

Children's Literature Cited

Ada, Alma Flor. 1993. *My Name Is Maria Isabel*. New York: Atheneum Books.

Alexander, Kwame. 2014. *The Crossover*. New York: Houghton Mifflin Harcourt.

Allen, Judy. 2003. *Are You a Snail?* Illustrated by Tudor Humphries. London: Kingfisher.

Anderson, Laurie Halse. 2008. *Independent Dames*. Illustrated by Matt Faulkner. New York: Simon and Schuster Books for Young Readers.

Applegate, Katherine. 2007. *Home of the Brave*. New York: Square Fish.

———. 2012. *The One and Only Ivan*. New York: HarperCollins.

———. 2017. *Wishtree*. New York: Feiwel and Friends.

Aston, Dianna Hutts. 2014a. *An Egg Is Quiet*. Illustrated by Sylvia Long. San Francisco: Chronicle Books.

———. 2014b. *A Seed Is Sleepy*. Illustrated by Sylvia Long. San Francisco: Chronicle Books.

———. 2015a. *A Butterfly Is Patient*. Illustrated by Sylvia Long. San Francisco: Chronicle Books.

———. 2015b. *A Rock Is Lively*. Illustrated by Sylvia Long. San Francisco: Chronicle Books.

———. 2017. *A Nest Is Noisy*. Illustrated by Sylvia Long. San Francisco: Chronicle Books.

Barnett, Mac. 2012. *Extra Yarn*. Illustrated by Jon Klassen. New York: Balzer and Bray.

Bennett, Kelly. 2008. *Not Norman*. Illustrated by Noah Z. Jones. Somerville, MA: Candlewick.

Boelts, Maribeth. 2009. *Those Shoes*. Illustrated by Noah Z. Jones. Somerville, MA: Candlewick.

Brown, Peter. 2013. *Mr. Tiger Goes Wild*. New York: Little, Brown.

Cannon, Janell. 1993. *Stellaluna*. New York: Houghton Mifflin Harcourt.

Cartaya, Pablo. 2018. *The Epic Fail of Arturo Zamora*. New York: Puffin Books.

Chin, Jason. 2012. *Island: A Story of the Galápagos*. New York: Roaring Brook.

———. 2016. *Coral Reef*. New York: Square Fish.

Cleary, Beverly. 2015. *Ribsy*. New York: HarperCollins.

Cornwell, Gaia. 2017. *Jabari Jumps*. Somerville, MA: Candlewick.

de la Peña, Matt. 2015. *Last Stop on Market Street*. Illustrated by Christian Robinson. New York: G. P. Putnam's Sons.

DiCamillo, Kate. 2000. *Because of Winn-Dixie*. Somerville, MA: Candlewick.

———. 2011a. *The Magician's Elephant*. Somerville, MA: Candlewick.

———. 2011b. *Mercy Watson Thinks Like a Pig*. Illustrated by Chris Van Dusen. Somerville, MA: Candlewick.

———. 2018. *Louisiana's Way Home*. Somerville, MA: Candlewick.

Doerrfeld, Cori. 2018. *The Rabbit Listened*. New York: Dial Books.

Draper, Sharon. 2010. *Out of My Mind*. New York: Atheneum Books.

Garcia, Rita Williams. 2010. *One Crazy Summer*. New York: Amistad.

Glaser, Karina Yan. 2017. *The Vanderbeekers of 141st Street*. New York: Houghton Mifflin Harcourt.

Godkin, Celia. 2006. *Wolf Island*. Markham, ON: Fitzhenry and Whiteside.

Gratz, Alan. 2017. *Refugee*. New York: Scholastic.

Grimes, Nikki. 2010. *Make Way for Dyamonde Daniel*. Illustrated by R. Gregory Christie. New York: Puffin Books.

Hesse, Karen. 1999. *Out of the Dust*. New York: Scholastic.

Jenkins, Steve. 2016. *Down, Down, Down: A Journey to the Bottom of the Sea*. New York: Knopf Books.

Johnson, Varian. 2014. *The Great Greene Heist*. New York: Arthur A. Levine Books.

Korman, Gordon. 2012. *Ungifted*. New York: Balzer and Bray.

Lai, Thanhha. 2013. *Inside Out and Back Again*. New York: HarperCollins.

Lee, JiHyeon. 2015. *Pool*. San Francisco: Chronicle Books.

———. 2018. *Door*. San Francisco: Chronicle Books.

Lewis, John, Andrew Aydin, and Nate Powell. 2016. *March*. Marietta, GA: Top Shelf Productions.

Lobel, Arnold. 1970. Frog and Toad series. New York: Harper and Row.

Lord, Cynthia. 2006. *Rules*. New York: Scholastic.

Lowry, Lois. 1989. *Number the Stars*. New York: Houghton Mifflin Harcourt.

Park, Linda Sue. 2011. *A Long Walk to Water*. New York: Houghton Mifflin Harcourt.

Pérez, Celia. 2018. *The First Rule of Punk*. New York: Puffin Books.

Polacco, Patricia. 2001. *The Keeping Quilt*. New York: Paula Wiseman Books.

Rawls, Wilson. 1961. *Where the Red Fern Grows*. New York: Yearling.

Reynolds, Jason. 2016. *Ghost*. New York: Atheneum Books.

Rhodes, Jewell Parker. 2018. *Ghost Boys*. New York: Little, Brown.

Ruurs, Margriet. 2016. *Stepping Stones.* Illustrated by Nizar Ali Badr. Victoria, BC: Orca Books.

Saeed, Aisha. 2018. *Amal Unbound.* New York: Nancy Paulsen Books.

Sanna, Francesca. 2016. *The Journey.* London: Flying Eye Books.

Schanzer, Rosalyn. 2007. *George vs. George.* Washington, DC: National Geographic Children's Books.

Simon, Seymour. 2002. *Super Storms.* San Francisco: Chronicle Books.

Sís, Peter. 1991. *Follow the Dream: The Story of Christopher Columbus.* New York: Knopf Books.

Thomas, Angie. 2017. *The Hate You Give.* New York: Balzer and Bray.

Waddell, Martin. 2002. *Owl Babies.* Illustrated by Patrick Benson. Somerville, MA: Candlewick.

Watson, Renee. 2017. *Piecing Me Together.* New York: Bloomsbury.

White, E. B. 2012. *Charlotte's Web.* New York: HarperCollins.

Wild, Margaret. 2006. *Fox.* La Jolla, CA: Kane Miller.

Winters, Kay. 2015. *Colonial Voices: Hear Them Speak.* New York: Puffin Books.

Wolk, Lauren. 2016. *Wolf Hollow.* New York: Puffin Books.

Woodson, Jacqueline. 2014. *Brown Girl Dreaming.* New York: Puffin Books.

Young, Rebecca. 2016. *Teacup.* Illustrated by Matt Otley. New York: Dial Books.

Works Cited

Achor, Shawn. 2018. *The Happiness Advantage: How a Positive Brain Fuels Success in Work and Life*. New York: Currency.

Alexander, Elizabeth. 2011. "Elizabeth Alexander: Words That Shimmer." Interview by Krista Tippett. *On Being* (podcast), January 6. https://onbeing.org/programs/elizabeth-alexander-words-that-shimmer/.

Alexander, Kwame. 2018. "Kwame Alexander and Cornelius Minor on the Heinemann Podcast." Interview by Cornelius Minor. *Heinemann Blog*, August 2. https://blog.heinemann.com/cornelius-minor-and-kwame-alexander-on-the-heinemann-podcast.

Allington, Richard. n.d. "We Could Teach All Children to Read." PowerPoint presentation. www.wmich.edu/conferencemanagement/rrcm/2015Downloads/WeCouldTeachAll ChildrenToRead_MI.pptx.

Allington, Richard, and Rachael E. Gabriel. 2012. "Every Child, Every Day." *Educational Leadership* 69 (6): 10–15.

Allyn, Pam. 2014. "Read Aloud. Change the World." *HuffPost*, May 3. www.huffingtonpost.com/pam-allyn/read-aloud-change-the-wor_b_4892116.html.

Anderson, Richard, Elfrieda H. Hiebert, Judith A. Scott, and Ian A. G. Wilkinson. 1985. *Becoming a Nation of Readers: The Report of the Commission of Reading*. Washington, DC: National Institute of Education.

Bassett, Katherine, Brett Bigham, and Laurie Calvert, eds. 2017. *Social Justice Book List.* Philadelphia, PA: National Network of State Teachers of the Year.

Bloomgarden-Smoke, Kara. 2013. "Let the Great World Tell Stories: Colum McCann and Esquire Celebrate Narrative 4 Launch." *Observer*, June 4. https://observer.com /2013/06/let-the-great-world-tell-stories-colum-mccann-and-esquire-celebrate -narrative-4-launch/.

Brown, Brene. 2010. "The Power of Vulnerability." TEDx video. Filmed June 2010 in Houston, Texas. www.ted.com/talks/brene_brown_on_vulnerability/transcript ?language=en#t-10035.

———. 2012. "Listening to Shame." TED video. Filmed March 2012 in Long Beach, California. www.ted.com/talks/brene_brown_listening_to_shame/transcript ?language=en#t-12356.

———. 2017. *Braving the Wilderness: The Quest for True Belonging and the Courage to Stand Alone.* New York: Random House.

Calkins, Lucy, and Mary Ehrenworth. 2015. *Historical Fiction Clubs.* Unit 4, Units of Study for Teaching Reading, Grade 4: A Workshop Curriculum, by Lucy Calkins and colleagues. Portsmouth, NH: Heinemann.

———. 2017. *A Guide to the Reading Workshop: Middle School Grades.* Unit 1, Units of Study for Teaching Reading, Middle School Grades, by Lucy Calkins and colleagues. Portsmouth, NH: Heinemann.

Calkins, Lucy, and Kathleen Tolan. 2015. *Building a Reading Life: Stamina, Fluency, and Engagement.* Unit 1, Units of Study for Teaching Reading, Grade 3: A Workshop Curriculum, by Lucy Calkins and colleagues. Portsmouth, NH: Heinemann.

Cardinali, Emily. 2018. "How to Make a Civics Education Stick." *NPR Ed*, August 14. www.npr.org/2018/08/14/632666071/how-to-make-a-civics-education-stick.

Corrigan, Maureen. 2011. "How E. B. White Spun Charlotte's Web." Review of *The Story of Charlotte's Web: E. B. White's Eccentric Life in Nature and the Birth of an American Classic* by Michael Sims. *Fresh Air*, July 5. https://www.npr.org/2011/07/05/137452030 /how-e-b-white-spun-charlottes-web.

Denton, Paula. 2007. "Open-Ended Questions." Responsive Classroom. February 1. www .responsiveclassroom.org/open-ended-questions/.

DiCamillo, Kate. 2015. "Reading Aloud Binds Us Together in Unanticipated Ways." *The Washington Post*, November 18. https://www.washingtonpost.com/entertainment /books/kate-dicamillo-reading-aloud-binds-us-together-in-unanticipated-ways /2015/11/18/c880e32c-83be-11e5-8ba6-cec48b74b2a7_story.html?utm_term= .d8d7dcf843e3.

Eskey, Nicholas. 2018. "Nothing but Bic Pens Will Do for Latino Artist Raúl the Third." *The Beat*, March 22. www.comicsbeat.com/interview-nothing-but-bic-pens-will-do-for -latino-artist-raul-the-third/.

Fassler, Joe. 2015. "Lauren Groff on Writing with Lightness." *The Atlantic*, October 6. https:// www.theatlantic.com/entertainment/archive/2015/10/by-heart-lauren-groff-virginia -woolf-time-passes/409045/.

Fisher, Douglas, and Nancy Frey. 2014. "Speaking Volumes." *Educational Leadership* 72 (3): 18–23.

Fox, Mem. 2001. *Reading Magic: Why Reading Aloud to Our Children Will Change Their Lives Forever*. Boston: Houghton Mifflin Harcourt.

Franklin, Ruth. 2018. "Tracy K. Smith, America's Poet Laureate, Is a Woman with a Mission." *The New York Times*, April 10. https://www.nytimes.com/2018/04/10 /magazine/tracy-k-smith-believes-america-needs-a-poetry-cure.html.

Gallagher, Kelly. 2009. *Readicide: How Schools Are Killing Reading and What You Can Do About It*. Portland, ME: Stenhouse.

Gawande, Atul. 2018. "Curiosity and What Equality Really Means." *The New Yorker*, June 2. https://www.newyorker.com/news/news-desk/curiosity-and-the-prisoner.

Gilbert, Elizabeth. 2015. *Big Magic: Creative Living Beyond Fear*. New York: Penguin.

———. 2016. "Elizabeth Gilbert: Choosing Curiosity Over Fear." Interview by Krista Tippett. *On Being* (podcast), July 7. https://onbeing.org/programs/elizabeth-gilbert -choosing-curiosity-over-fear-may2018/.

Griss, Susan. 2013. "The Power of Movement in Teaching and Learning." *Education Week*, March 20. https://www.edweek.org/tm/articles/2013/03/19/fp_griss.html.

Groff, Lauren. 2015. "Write Like a Shark: An Interview with Lauren Groff." Interview by S. Tremaine Nelson. *The Common Online*, September 6. www.thecommononline.org /write-like-a-shark-an-interview-with-lauren-groff/.

———. 2016a. "How Two Novels Became One, *In the Shape of a Marriage*." *The Guardian*, July 5. https://www.theguardian.com/books/2016/jul/05/lauren-groff-how-two-novels -became-one-in-the-shape-of-a-marriage.

———. 2016b. "Sean Penn, Pt. 2; Lauren Groff." Interview by Charlie Rose. *Charlie Rose* (television show), January 19. https://charlierose.com/episodes/23391?autoplay=true.

Haby, Gracia. 2014. "Dance Is Music Made Visible." *High Up in the Trees* (blog), July 7. https:// gracialouise.typepad.com/high_up_in_the_trees/2014/07/dance-is-music-made -visible.html.

Hammond, Zaretta. 2013a. "Cultural Responsiveness Starts with Real Caring." *Teaching Tolerance*, February 8. www.tolerance.org/magazine/cultural-responsiveness-starts -with-real-caring.

———. 2013b. "Five Things Not to Do During Black History Month: Careful Planning, Thoughtfulness and Alliances Will Help Educators Avoid the Pitfalls of Black History Month." *Teaching Tolerance*, March 6. www.tolerance.org/print/76882/print.

———. 2015. "Is Implicit Bias Racist? Three Things Every Teacher Should Know About Implicit Bias and the Brain." *Teaching Tolerance*, June 1. www.tolerance.org/magazine /is-implicit-bias-racist.

Harris, Aisha. 2018. "Kerry Washington Has Something to Fear." *The New York Times*, October 24, 7. https://www.nytimes.com/2018/10/24/theater/kerry-washington -american-son-broadway.html.

International Literacy Association. 2018. *The Power and Promise of Read-Alouds and Independent Reading*. Literacy leadership brief. Newark, DE: Author. https://literacy-worldwide.org/docs/default-source/where-we-stand/ila-power-promise-read -alouds-independent-reading.pdf.

Isherwood, Charles. 2013. "What Makes a Great Shakespearean?" *The New York Times*, November 17, 6. https://www.nytimes.com/2013/11/17/theater/mark-rylance-and-other-shakespeareans-at-work.html.

———. 2015. "Review: *The Absolute Brightness of Leonard Pelkey*, James Lecesne's One-Man Play." *The New York Times*, February 22, C4. https://www.nytimes.com/2015/02/23/theater/review-the-absolute-brightness-of-leonard-pelkey-james-lecesnes-one-man-play.html.

Kachka, Boris. 2015. "Writer-Actor James Lecesne Morphs into 9 of His Characters." *New York Magazine*, July 13. https://www.nytimes.com/2015/02/23/theater/review-the-absolute-brightness-of-leonard-pelkey-james-lecesnes-one-man-play.html.

Kaphar, Titus. 2017. "Can Art Amend History?" TED video. Filmed April 2017 in Vancouver, British Columbia. www.ted.com/talks/titus_kaphar_can_art_amend_history#t-10562.

Keene, Ellin Oliver. 2012. *Talk About Understanding: Rethinking Classroom Talk to Enhance Comprehension*. Portsmouth, NH: Heinemann.

Keene, Ellin, and Tom Newkirk. 2017. "Ellin Keene Reflects on *Mosaic of Thought*'s 20th Anniversary with Tom Newkirk." *Heinemann Blog*, July 14. https://blog.heinemann.com/podcast-ellin-keene-with-tom-newkirk-1.

Laminack, Lester. 2016. *The Ultimate Read-Aloud Resource: Making Every Moment Intentional and Instructional with Best Friends Books*. New York: Scholastic.

Landay, Eileen, and Kurt Wootton. 2012. *A Reason to Read: Linking Literacy and the Arts*. Cambridge, MA: Harvard Education Press.

Lawrence, Vanessa. 2016. "Amandla Stenberg Is Coming to Terms with Being a Revolutionary." *W Magazine*, July 6. https://www.wmagazine.com/story/amandla-stenberg-hunger-games-instagram.

Lehman, Christopher, and Kate Roberts. 2013. *Falling in Love with Close Reading: Lessons for Analyzing Texts—and Life*. Portsmouth, NH: Heinemann.

Levinson, Amy. 2017. "Leading with Humor: An Interview with Feiffer's *A Funny Thing Happened on the Way to the Gynecologic Oncology Unit at Memorial Sloan Kettering Cancer Center of New York City*'s Playwright and Actor Halley Feiffer." *Geffen*

Playhouse News, August 21. https://blog.geffenplayhouse.org/leading-with-humor-e2cf9127e870.

Lincoln Center Education. n.d. "Capacities for Imaginative Learning Thinking: LCE's Approach to Arts Education." https://lincolncentereducation.org/about#start.

Ma, Yo-Yo. 2014. "Yo-Yo Ma: Music Happens Between the Notes." Interview by Krista Tippett. *On Being* (podcast), September 4. https://onbeing.org/programs/yo-yo-ma-music-happens-between-the-notes-jul2018/.

Macaulay, Alastair. 2018. "City Ballet's 'Robbins 100': Making Musical Theater." *The New York Times*, May 22. https://www.nytimes.com/2018/05/22/arts/dance/new-york-city-ballet-robbins-100.html.

Mead, Rebecca. 2015. "All About the Hamiltons." *The New Yorker*, Feb. 9. https://www.newyorker.com/magazine/2015/02/09/hamiltons.

Miller, Donalyn. 2009. *The Book Whisperer: Awakening the Inner Reader in Every Child*. San Francisco: Jossey-Bass.

———. 2016. "Never Too Old: Reading Aloud to Independent Readers." *On Our Minds* (blog), February 11. http://oomscholasticblog.com/post/never-too-old-reading-aloud-independent-readers-donalyn-miller.

Millner, Denene. 2018. "Black Kids Don't Want to Read About Harriet Tubman All the Time." *The New York Times*, March 11, 10. https://www.nytimes.com/2018/03/10/opinion/sunday/children-literature-books-blacks.html.

Minor, Cornelius, and Jamie Richard. 2018. "Championing Social Justice and Equity in Your School." Ed Current (Newsela webinar session), August 14.

Neville, Morgan (director). 2018. *Won't You Be My Neighbor?* Los Angeles: Tremolo Productions.

Nye, Naomi Shihab. 2016. "Naomi Shihabe Nye: Your Life Is a Poem." Interview by host Krista Tippett. *On Being* (podcast), July 28. YourLifeIsaPoem.mp3. https://onbeing.org/programs/naomi-shihab-nye-your-life-is-a-poem-mar2018/.

O'Donohue, John. 2008. "John O'Donohue: The Inner Landscape of Beauty." Interview by Krista Tippett. *On Being* (podcast), February 28. https://onbeing.org/programs/john-odonohue-the-inner-landscape-of-beauty-aug2017/.

Ozma, Alice. 2012. *The Reading Promise: My Father and the Books We Shared.* New York: Grand Central.

Park, Linda Sue. 2015. "Can a Children's Book Change the World?" TEDx video. Filmed November 14, 2015, in Brookline, Massachusetts. www.youtube.com/watch?v =40xz0afCjnM.

Paulson, Michael. 2018. "How Orin Wolf Orchestrated a Tony Coup with *A Band's Visit.*" *The New York Times,* June 11. https://www.nytimes.com/2018/06/11/theater/the-bands -visit-orin-wolf-tony-wins.html.

Pierson, Joanne Marttila. 2019. "Frequently Asked Questions." University of Michigan Dyslexia Help. http://dyslexiahelp.umich.edu/answers/faq.

Poetry Foundation. Naomi Shihab Nye. https://www.poetryfoundation.org/poets/naomi -shihab-nye.

Powers, Kevin. 2018. "What Kept Me from Killing Myself." *The New York Times,* June 17, SR5. https://www.nytimes.com/2018/06/16/opinion/sunday/books-saved-me-from -suicide.html.

Pranikoff, Kara. 2017. *Teaching Talk: A Practical Guide to Fostering Student Thinking and Conversation.* Portsmouth, NH: Heinemann.

Rasinski, Timothy. 2012. "Why Reading Fluency Should Be Hot!" *The Reading Teacher* 65 (8): 516–22.

Ripp, Pernille. 2015. "Why Picture Books—5 Reasons They Belong in Every Classroom." *Pernille Ripp* (blog), July 30. https://pernillesripp.com/2015/07/30/why-picture-books -5-reasons-why-they-belong-in-every-classroom/.

Robinson, Ken, and Lou Aronica. 2015. *Creative Schools: The Grassroots Revolution That's Transforming Education.* New York: Penguin.

Roy, Jessica. 2016. "11 Year Old 'Sick of Reading About White Boys and Dogs' Starts Her Own Black Girl Book Drive." *The Cut* (blog), January 22. https://www.thecut.com /2016/01/girl-starts-1000blackgirlbooks-book-drive.html.

Safi, Omid. 2014. "The Disease of Being Busy." *On Being* (blog), November 6. https:// onbeing.org/blog/the-disease-of-being-busy/.

Salzberg, Sharon. 2004. "The Power of Intention." *O, the Oprah Magazine*, January. http://www.oprah.com/spirit/sharon-salzberg-the-power-of-intention/all.

Sandberg, Cheryl. 2017. "How to Build Resilient Kids, Even After a Loss." *The New York Times*, April 24, A23. https://www.nytimes.com/2017/04/24/opinion/sheryl-sandberg-how-to-build-resilient-kids-even-after-a-loss.html.

Scharf, Amy. 2016. *Critical Practices for Anti-bias Education*. Montgomery, AL: Teaching Tolerance.

Serravallo, Jennifer. 2015. "Jennifer Serravallo: Focusing on Engagement." *Heinemann Blog*, January 22. https://blog.heinemann.com/jenniferserravallofocusingonengagement.

———. 2018. *Understanding Texts and Readers: Responsive Comprehension Instruction with Leveled Texts*. Portsmouth, NH: Heinemann.

Smith, Frank. 1987. *Joining the Literacy Club: Further Essays into Education*. Portsmouth, NH: Heinemann.

Strauss, Valerie. 2015a. "Great Books That Inspire Love of Reading in Kids—Recommended by Kids." *Washington Post*, April 2. www.washingtonpost.com/news/answer-sheet/wp/2015/04/02/great-books-that-inspire-a-love-of-reading-in-kids-recommended-by-kids/?utm_term=.f88061d3c062.

———. 2015b. "Why Kids Still Need 'Real Books' to Read—and Time in School to Enjoy Them." *Washington Post*, October 17. www.washingtonpost.com/news/answer-sheet/wp/2015/10/17/why-kids-still-need-real-books-to-read-and-time-in-school-to-enjoy-them/?utm_term=.b92a6f95490b.

Trelease, Jim. 2013. *The Read-Aloud Handbook*. New York: Penguin.

Turkle, Sherry. 2012. "The Flight from Conversation." *The New York Times*, April 21. https://www.nytimes.com/2012/04/22/opinion/sunday/the-flight-from-conversation.html.

Vercelletto, Christina. 2018. "Never Too Old: Embracing Picture Books to Teach Older Students." *School Library Journal*, February 23. www.slj.com/?detailStory=never-old-embracing-picture-books-teach-older-students.

Watson, Renée. 2017. *Piecing Me Together*. New York: Bloomsbury.

Wilhelm, Jeffrey, and Chris Butts. 2018. "Moving Teachers and Students Toward Joyful and Expert Reading: A Conversation with Jeffrey Wilhelm and Chris Butts." Interview by Jennifer D. Turner. *Language Arts* 95 (6): 383–88.

Wilkinson, Alec. 2012. "Stage Secret." *The New Yorker*, May 21. https://www.newyorker.com/magazine/2012/05/21/stage-secret.

Winerip, Michael. 2010. "A Father Daughter Bond, Page by Page." *The New York Times*, March 18. https://www.nytimes.com/2010/03/21/fashion/21GenB.html.

Wolk, Steven. 2010. "What Should Students Read?" *Phi Delta Kappan* 91 (7): 9–16.

Zander, Benjamin. 2017. "Benjamin Zander: How Does Music Transform Us?" Interview by Guy Raz. *NPR TED Radio Hour*, November 10. https://www.npr.org/templates/transcript/transcript.php?storyId=562884481.

Zimmer, Carl. 2018. "'Lifeboats' Amid the World's Wildfires." *The New York Times*, October 12. www.nytimes.com/2018/10/12/science/wildfire-biodiversity.html.